SUPERCHARGED TO SOAR

David S. Philemon

Royal Diadem Publishing Inc.

Copyright © 2024 David S. Philemon

All rights reserved. First Edition 2024.
Printed in the USA.

Published by David S. Philemon and Royal Diadem Publishing Inc.

All rights reserved under International Copyright Law. No part of this book may be reproduced, stored in a retrieval system, or transmitted in any form or by any means, electronic, mechanical, photocopying, recording, or otherwise, the express written permission from the author and publisher. Unauthorized use or distribution of this material is strictly prohibited.

Supercharged To Soar
978-1-966141-58-7

For permissions, additional information, or bulk order inquiries, please contact the author.

Write:
Royal Diadem Publishing Inc.
4836 W. 13th Street, Cicero, IL 60804
1 (312) 970-0183

Unless otherwise indicated, all Scripture quotations in this volume are taken from the King James Version (KJV) and the New King James Version (NKJV) of the Holy Bible.

To the Almighty God, my foundation and ever-present help. I am grateful for Your boundless love and grace that sustain me daily. And to my mentor in ministry, Rev. George Izunwa, whose steadfast commitment to the call of God has deeply impacted my life. Your guidance and support have been invaluable, encouraging me to walk boldly in the path God has set before me. Thank you for your example and your heart for the Kingdom.

ACKNOWLEDGMENT

This book would not have been possible without the unwavering support, dedication, and talent of an extraordinary team. My deepest gratitude goes to each of you for your contributions, insights, and encouragement throughout this journey.

First and foremost, thank you to Rev. Mimi Philemon my dear wife, Rev. Shina Gentry, and and my assistant pastor Rev. Bright Amudoaghan for your incredible effort, encouragement, and belief in this project. Your support has been instrumental in bringing this vision to life.

To the dedicated leaders of Royal Diadem Publishing, Ide Imogie and Kishawna Bailey, I am immensely grateful for your belief in this project from the very beginning and for investing your time and energy into its development. Your creativity, dedication, and expertise have been the backbone of this endeavor.

I am especially grateful to the Royal Diadem Publishing team—Beulah Orogun, Emmanuella Ben-Eboh, Doyinsade Awodele, Kim Matthews, and Shante Gill, for your meticulous attention to detail, refining every page and ensuring that each word reflects our vision.

A heartfelt thank you to my family, friends, and colleagues whose unwavering support and belief in this project gave me the courage and strength to see it through.

Finally, thank you to all the readers and supporters who make this work meaningful. I am humbled and honored to share this journey with each of you.

With all my gratitude,
David Philemon

CONTENTS

Title Page
Copyright
Dedication
Acknowledgment

INTRODUCTION	1
PART 1	6
GOD'S BUSINESS OF PUTTING THINGS RIGHT	7
CHAPTER 1	8
THE RIGHTEOUS LORD LOVES WHAT IS RIGHT AND JUST	9
CHAPTER 2	14
THE WORK OF GOD IN OUR LIVES	15
CHAPTER 3	22
BREAKTHROUGH IN THE FAMILY LINEAGE	23
CHAPTER 4	30
TRUSTING GOD'S PLAN FOR THE IMPOSSIBLE	31
PART 2	37
RECONNECTING WITH GOD'S VOICE AND SPIRITUAL AUTHORITY	38
CHAPTER 5	39
RESTORING THE VOICE OF GOD IN YOUR LIFE	40
CHAPTER 6	45

THE POWER OF SPIRITUAL VISION AND INTERVENTION	46
CHAPTER 7	54
BECOMING A FORCE IN THE SPIRITUAL REALM	55
PART 3	63
RISING ABOVE LIFE'S CHALLENGES	64
CHAPTER 8	65
CONQUERING THE CONTRADICTIONS OF YOUR PAST	66
CHAPTER 9	75
THE BATTLE FOR YOUR DESTINY	76
CHAPTER 10	86
UNDERSTANDING THE SPIRITUAL WARFARE AROUND YOU	87
CHAPTER 11	94
CUTTING OFF THE CANCEROUS FORCES IN YOUR LIFE	95
PART 4	104
EMBRACING YOUR SUPERNATURAL CALLING	105
CHAPTER 12	106
RISING TO YOUR FULL POTENTIAL IN GOD	107
CHAPTER 13	111
LIVING AS A SPIRITUAL POWERHOUSE	112
CHAPTER 14	120
BECOMING AN UNSTOPPABLE FORCE FOR GOD'S GLORY	121
CONCLUSION	130
A SPECIAL CALL TO SALVATION & NEW BEGINNINGS FROM APOSTLE DR. DAVID PHILEMON	136
APPENDIX	138
ABOUT THE BOOK	142

INTRODUCTION

Embracing God's Power To Soar

Have you ever felt like there's more to life than what you're experiencing right now? Have you ever wondered if there's a greater purpose for you—something that stretches beyond your current circumstances, beyond your struggles, and beyond your limitations? This feeling, this longing for more, is a natural part of the human experience. Deep inside, we know that we were created for something greater. The good news is that God has designed us to soar—to rise above the challenges and obstacles of life and fulfill the incredible purpose He has planned for us. The question is: How do we embrace that power and soar like we were meant to? In life, we often face situations that seem impossible. We struggle with feelings of inadequacy, doubt, and fear. These challenges can make us feel stuck, as if we're grounded, unable to reach the heights we know we're meant to. But here's the truth: God's power is available to you to help you break free from those limits and soar. With God's strength, you are not meant to stay on the ground—you're meant to rise and fly, to live a life of victory and purpose.

God's Word is filled with promises of His strength, His help, and His ability to empower us to rise above anything that stands in our way. As believers, we are never meant to face life's challenges alone. The power of God is always available to us, enabling us to overcome, to grow, and to achieve the impossible. The Bible teaches us that God is our source of strength. We don't have to rely on our own power, which is limited and weak. Instead, we can tap into the unlimited, supernatural strength of God. Isaiah 40:31, "But those who wait on the Lord shall renew their strength; they shall mount up with wings like eagles, they shall run and not be weary, they shall walk and not faint." This powerful verse gives us a beautiful picture of what happens when we rely on God. When we trust in Him, He gives us the strength to rise like eagles. The eagle is known for its ability to soar high above the storm, flying above the clouds and the challenges below. God promises that, through Him, we can soar above our troubles and limitations. But what does it mean to "wait on the Lord" and how do we embrace God's power to soar?

To soar, we must first acknowledge that it is God who gives us the strength. In our human weakness, it's easy to forget that we don't have to do everything on our own. God doesn't expect us to figure out life's struggles by ourselves. Instead, He invites us to come to Him in trust and dependence. In Psalm 28:7, David writes: "The Lord is my strength and my shield; my heart trusted in Him, and I am helped; therefore my heart greatly rejoices, and with my song I will praise Him." David understood that God was his strength and shield. He trusted in God, and because of that, he was helped. This trust is what allows us to tap into God's power to soar. When we rely on God's strength, we are not weighed down by our problems, but we rise above them. The challenges we face are real. Whether it's emotional struggles, financial hardship, health issues, or relationship problems, these difficulties can weigh us down. But God's Word assures us that He gives us the strength to overcome. Our ability to rise above life's challenges doesn't come from our own strength. It comes from Christ, who empowers us. When we rely on Him, there is nothing we cannot overcome. He gives us the strength to soar through difficult circumstances, not by our own power, but by His supernatural ability. While God promises to give us the strength to soar, we must also take action. Soaring isn't passive. The eagle doesn't just wait for the wind to lift it into the sky; it actively spreads its wings and uses the wind to lift it higher. Similarly, we must take the steps of faith to rise above our circumstances. As we step out in faith, God empowers us to soar to new heights. When we embrace God's power, we are transformed. We move from a place of fear, doubt, and limitation to a place of strength, confidence, and purpose. God's power gives us the ability to rise above our challenges and live a life that reflects His glory. Ephesians 6:10, "Finally, my brethren, be strong in the Lord and in the power of His might." This is the key to soaring—being strong in the Lord, not in ourselves. When we allow God's power to work in and through us, we are able to soar far beyond what we ever imagined.

God has a purpose for your life that goes beyond just getting by or living day-to-day. Too many people settle into the "status quo," which means simply doing what's comfortable and familiar without aiming higher or pushing for growth. But when you understand and embrace God's purpose for you, everything changes. You begin to move toward something greater, something more fulfilling, and you will never be the same again. God's purpose for you is more than just a general idea. He has specific plans for you that are good, meaningful, and filled with hope. In the Bible, in Jeremiah 29:11, "For I know the plans I have for you, plans to prosper you and not to harm you, plans to give you a hope and a future." This verse reminds us that God's plans are good, and He wants us to succeed and live with purpose. His purpose for your life is connected to your unique gifts, talents, and passions. It's about using what He has given you to make a difference in the world around you. This might include serving others, living out your faith boldly, or accomplishing goals that help build His kingdom. Moving beyond the status quo means stepping into that bigger purpose and letting it shape everything you do.

There are several reasons why people stay stuck in the status quo.

For some, it's fear—fear of failure, fear of change, or fear of the unknown. For others, it might be comfort—living in a routine is familiar and easy, and it's hard to take the risk of stepping out into something different. Some people simply don't know what else is possible or don't feel they have the strength or resources to move beyond where they are.

But God didn't create you to settle. 2 Corinthians 5:17 says, "Therefore, if anyone is in Christ, the new creation has come: The old has gone, the new is here!" God wants to transform your life. You were made to grow, to stretch, and to move forward, not stay in one place. When you understand this truth, it empowers you to take the steps necessary to move beyond the status quo. Each person is created for a specific purpose. This could be in your job, your family, your church, or in the community. God already has work prepared for you to do, and it's time to step into it. Moving beyond the status quo means embracing change and growth. God wants to shape you into the person He created you to be. This might mean stepping out of your comfort zone, learning new skills, or letting go of old habits. As you grow in your relationship with God, you will see changes in your mindset, your character, and your abilities. Romans 12:2, "be transformed by the renewing of your mind." God will renew your mind and equip you to do His will. God's purpose for your life will unfold in His perfect timing. It may not happen all at once, but as you stay faithful and trust in Him, He will guide your steps. Be patient and trust that God is working behind the scenes, preparing you for the future He has for you.

Living with purpose is an exciting journey. When you move beyond the status quo, you enter into the adventure that God has prepared for you. You don't have to settle for ordinary when God has extraordinary plans for you. Embrace His calling, take the next step in faith, and watch as He opens doors, breaks chains, and leads you into a life that is full of purpose, joy, and victory. Remember, you were created for something greater than simply getting by. God has a plan for you, and it's time to step into it.

Move beyond the status quo, and experience the fullness of God's purpose for your life! God has called you to soar, to rise above the difficulties of life, and to fulfill the incredible purpose He has for you. You don't have to stay grounded by fear, doubt, or circumstances. God's power is available to you, and by trusting in Him, you can rise above it all. Embrace His strength, trust in His promises, and take bold steps of faith. As you do, you will experience the freedom and victory that come from soaring in the power of God. Are you ready to embrace the power of God and soar? The choice is yours, and the strength is already available. Let go of your limitations and rise to the heights God has prepared for you. He has given you everything you need to rise above the difficulties of life and to walk in His victory. Through His strength, you can overcome every obstacle, defeat every enemy, and live the life He has destined for you. Trust in His power, embrace His grace, and let Him lead you to new heights. With God's strength, you are supercharged to soar.

PART 1

GOD'S BUSINESS OF PUTTING THINGS RIGHT

"God is not a divine being who is unconcerned with the world; He is a Father, a redeemer, working to restore what was lost, to heal what was broken, and to bring all things into their proper order." C.S. Lewis, Mere Christianity

"And we know that in all things God works for the good of those who love him, who have been called according to his purpose." Romans 8:28

CHAPTER 1

THE RIGHTEOUS LORD LOVES WHAT IS RIGHT AND JUST

The term "righteous" refers to something that is good, right, and just. When we say the "righteous Lord," we are talking about God who always does what is good, fair, and right. He is perfect in His actions and decisions. He doesn't make mistakes or show favoritism. God's righteousness means that He is always just in everything He does, and He wants to see justice and fairness in the world. In Psalm 11:7, we read, "For the righteous Lord loves justice; the upright will see his face." This verse helps us understand an important truth about God: He loves what is right and just. It about God's nature—how He cares deeply about fairness, righteousness, and justice. Let's break it down in simple terms to understand what this means for us today. When the Bible says that God "loves justice," it means that He cares deeply about what is fair. He does not like injustice, wrongdoing, or unfairness. If something is unfair or harmful to others, God does not approve of it. He wants to make things right and restore balance. God's love for justice is also shown through His desire for people to live righteous lives—doing what is right according to His commands.

In practical terms, this means that God calls us to live in ways that reflect His righteousness. We are to treat others fairly, act justly, and stand up for what is right, even when it's difficult. God wants us to be people who love justice just as He does.

The second part of Psalm 11:7 says, *"The upright will see his face."* This refers to the idea that those who live righteous lives, seeking justice and doing what is right, will experience God's presence. To "see His face" means to be in close fellowship with God, to experience His peace, and to receive His blessings. It's a beautiful promise that God will draw near to those who live justly and uprightly. Living a life that is upright means living with honesty, integrity, and a desire to do good. It doesn't mean being perfect, but it means striving to do what's right with a sincere heart. When we live this way, we can trust that God will honor us with His presence and guidance. As believers, we are called to reflect God's character. If God loves what is right and just, we should also strive to love what is right and just. This affects every part of our lives —how we treat others, how we stand up for fairness, and how we live out our faith. In all our dealings, whether at home, school, work, or in the community, we should always be fair and honest. God values truth, so we must live with integrity. God cares about justice for the poor, the oppressed, and the vulnerable. As His followers, we should care about these people too. We should speak up for those who cannot speak for themselves. Justice isn't just about laws and rules; it's also about showing kindness and mercy. We should act with love and compassion toward others, just as God shows mercy to us. Striving to live a righteous life means having a heart that desires to do what is right. We should avoid sin and seek to live in ways that please God, knowing that He loves and honors those who seek righteousness. Sometimes, we may feel that things aren't fair or that evil is winning. But we can trust that God will set things right in His time. He is a just God, and He will always bring justice in the end.

Understanding God's Heart For Justice And Righteousness

Justice means treating everyone fairly and ensuring that people get what they deserve. It involves making things right when they are wrong. God's justice is perfect, meaning He always does what is fair and right. In the Bible, we see that God hates injustice and loves when people do what is right. Righteousness means being right with God. It involves living according to His laws and ways. When someone is righteous, they live in a way that pleases God. Righteousness is not about being perfect but about seeking to live in a way that honors God and reflects His character. God is deeply concerned about justice. He wants to make sure that the poor, the oppressed, and the powerless are treated fairly. In Isaiah 1:17, God tells His people, *"Learn to do good. Seek justice, help the oppressed, defend the cause of orphans, fight for the rights of widows."* This verse shows that justice is about more than just following rules; it's about caring for people who may not be able to defend themselves and making sure everyone is treated fairly. God's heart for righteousness is seen in how He calls His people to live. He wants them to be just, kind, and fair in all their dealings. Micah 6:8, *"He has shown you, O mortal, what is good. And what does the Lord require of you? To act justly and to love mercy and to walk humbly with your God."* This verse shows that God desires His people to live with justice, mercy, and humility. God's righteousness also means that He wants His people to seek Him first and live according to His truth. In Matthew 6:33, Jesus , *"But seek first His kingdom and His righteousness, and all these things will be given to you as well."* When we seek God's righteousness, we put His will and ways first in our lives.

Jesus is the perfect example of God's heart for justice and righteousness. He came to earth to show people what it looks like to live righteously and to fight for justice. Jesus cared for the poor, healed the sick, and defended those who were treated unfairly. He came to bring justice to those who were oppressed and to bring righteousness by pointing people to God (Luke 4:18-19). We are called to treat everyone fairly and to stand up for those who cannot stand up for themselves. This means helping the poor, defending the oppressed, and making sure everyone is treated with dignity and respect. We should always strive to live in a way that pleases God. This means following His Word, being kind and loving, and doing what is right, even when it is hard. Just like Jesus, we are called to serve others, love our neighbors, and care for those in need. Jesus was the perfect example of how to live with justice and righteousness, and we should follow His example in our daily lives. We should pray for God's justice to be done in the world. We can pray for the poor, the oppressed, and the suffering, asking God to bring justice to those who are hurting.

How God Makes Things Right When Life Seems Out Of Order

Life can sometimes feel chaotic, like everything is out of place. Problems can arise suddenly, relationships can break down, and dreams can feel far out of reach. During these times, it can seem like things are beyond fixing, and we may wonder if anything can make things right again. But the Bible teaches us that God has the power to make things right, even when life seems completely out of order. God is in the business of restoring what is broken. Whether it's a relationship, a dream, or even your own heart, God has the ability to bring healing and wholeness. Joel 2:25 *"I will repay you for the years the locusts have eaten…"* This verse reminds us that even if life has taken something away, God can restore it and make it better than before. If you're feeling broken or lost, God promises that He can bring healing and make things whole again. When everything around us feels like a storm, God is the calm in the middle of it. God doesn't just fix our problems; He gives us His peace that helps us feel safe and secure, even when things aren't perfect. Sometimes, things happen that seem unfair or beyond our control. But God has the power to turn even bad situations around. (Romans 8:28). No matter what happens, God can use it for good in our lives. It may not always make sense at the time, but God can bring blessings and lessons even through tough times.

When we stray off course or make mistakes, God is always ready to help us find our way back. Psalm 23:3, *"He refreshes my soul. He guides me along the right paths for his name's sake."* God doesn't leave us alone when we go through difficult times; He gently leads us back to the right path, helping us make wise choices and giving us strength to move forward. He is a loving shepherd who guides His people with care and wisdom. Sometimes, it may feel like God is taking too long to fix things. But God works in His perfect timing, which is always better than our own. While we may want things to happen quickly, God knows exactly when to act to bring about His perfect plan. Trusting in His timing allows us to have peace and patience, knowing that God is working even when we can't see it. Sometimes, God doesn't just fix things on His own; He uses us to help restore and make things right. God has given us the opportunity to be a part of His work by helping others, restoring relationships, and bringing healing where there is pain. God works through us to make things right in the world. When everything feels out of order, God promises to be with us. No matter how out of control things may feel, God is always with us. He strengthens us, helps us, and holds us up, reminding us that we are never alone.

CHAPTER 2

THE WORK OF GOD IN OUR LIVES

In Job 41, God describes a creature called the Leviathan. The Bible paints a picture of this creature as something powerful, untamable, and fearsome. It's said to be a sea monster, almost indestructible, with scales so tough that no weapon can pierce them. The creature is described as having a fiery breath, sharp teeth, and a huge, powerful body. In many ways, the Leviathan symbolizes something that is beyond human control or understanding. While we may not fully know if the Leviathan was a real creature or if it represents something else, the point God is making is clear: God is in control of even the most powerful and mysterious parts of creation, and He has power over everything that seems uncontrollable or frightening. In the story of Job, Job is a righteous man who suffers many terrible things. He loses his health, his wealth, and his family, and he is left questioning why all of this is happening to him. Job, like many of us, wonders why life is hard and why bad things happen. In this moment, God speaks to Job, and part of what He says is about the Leviathan.
Through describing the Leviathan, God is teaching Job, and us, several important lessons about His work in our lives.

The Leviathan is a creature that no one can tame, no one can defeat, and no one can fully understand. God describes how no human can capture or control this creature, but He, as the

Creator, is the one who made it and rules over it. God's power is far greater than anything we can imagine or control. When we face challenges in life that feel too big or too powerful, it's a reminder that while we may not have control, God does. God is in control of everything in the world, including the things that seem impossible or overwhelming to us. He made the Leviathan, and He is able to handle anything that seems too strong for us.

Job 41:11, *"Who has a claim against me that I must pay? Everything under heaven belongs to me."* This reminds us that everything in our lives, even the tough situations, belongs to God. He is in charge and has the power to make things right. God doesn't always explain why things happen the way they do, just like He doesn't explain everything about the Leviathan. But the point is that God's wisdom and ways are much higher than ours. There are things we may never fully understand, but we can trust that God knows what He is doing. When we face difficulties or things we don't understand, we can remember that God sees the bigger picture. Even though we might not understand why things happen, we can trust that God is working for our good. Job 41 also shows us that no one can challenge God's strength. The Leviathan might be strong, but God is stronger. This teaches us that when we feel weak, when we face difficulties that we can't handle on our own, God's strength is enough for us. Even in our weakness, God's power is at work in us, and His strength is greater than any difficulty we may face. God shows Job that He is the Creator of all things, including creatures like the Leviathan. The purpose of everything in creation, including us, is to bring glory to God. Even in the hardest times of life, God is working to shape us and bring glory to His name. No matter what happens in our lives, God is using it to bring about good and to make us more like Jesus, who brings glory to God. God shows Job how small and powerless humans are compared to His mighty works. This isn't meant to discourage us, but to remind us that we are not alone. Just as God rules over the Leviathan, He rules over all things in our lives. We may not have control, but God does. Psalm 8:4-5, *"What is mankind that you are mindful of them, human beings that you care for them?*

You have made them a little lower than the angels and crowned them with glory and honor." Even though we are small compared to God's great power, He still cares for us deeply and works in our lives for our good.

God's Power Over Forces That Seem Insurmountable

God has limitless power. He is the Creator of the universe, and there is nothing too hard for Him. In Jeremiah 32:17, *"Ah, Sovereign Lord, you have made the heavens and the earth by your great power and outstretched arm. Nothing is too hard for you."* God who created everything we see can handle anything in our lives. Whether it's a personal problem or something that feels as big as the whole world, God's power is enough to overcome it. We hear many stories of God demonstrating His power over nature. For example, when the Israelites were fleeing Egypt and found themselves trapped between the Red Sea and Pharaoh's army, it seemed like an impossible situation. But God parted the sea, allowing His people to walk through on dry ground. (Exodus 14:21-22) What seemed like an insurmountable obstacle became a pathway to victory because of God's power. This story reminds us that when we face obstacles, we can trust God to make a way, even when it seems impossible. As Jesus said in Luke 18:27, *"What is impossible with man is possible with God."* Sometimes, the forces we face aren't physical but spiritual. We may feel attacked by fear, anxiety, or temptation. The Bible assures us that God is more powerful than any spiritual force. Ephesians 6:12, *"For our struggle is not against flesh and blood, but against the rulers, against the authorities, against the powers of this dark world and against the spiritual forces of evil in the heavenly realms."* When we feel under attack, we can call on God, who is stronger than any evil force. God has already defeated Satan through the death and resurrection of Jesus, and His power is available to help us overcome every spiritual battle.

Fear can sometimes feel like an insurmountable force. It can paralyze us, making it hard to take the next step in life. But God's power can break the grip of fear. Isaiah 41:10, *"So do not fear, for I am with you; do not be dismayed, for I am your God. I will strengthen you and help you; I will uphold you with my righteous right hand."* When we feel afraid, we can trust that God's power will carry us through. His presence gives us courage, and His promises give us peace. Sometimes, God asks us to step out in faith, even when we don't see how things will work out. In Matthew 17:20, , *"Truly I tell you, if you have faith as small as a mustard seed, you can say to this mountain, 'Move from here to there,' and it will move. Nothing will be impossible for you."* This doesn't mean we will never face difficulties, but it does mean that God's power can help us overcome them. Even a small amount of faith connects us to a God who can do great things. One of the most amazing things about God's power is that it shows up when we feel weak. When we feel like we can't go on, God's strength becomes our strength. He helps us to keep moving forward, even when we feel like giving up. This is why the apostle Paul could say, *"When I am weak, then I am strong."* (2 Corinthians 12:10) It's not our own strength that gets us through tough times—it's God's power working in us. The ultimate enemy that feels insurmountable is death itself. But Jesus conquered death when He rose from the grave. 1 Corinthians 15:55-57, *"Where, O death, is your victory? Where, O death, is your sting? ... But thanks be to God! He gives us the victory through our Lord Jesus Christ."* Because of Jesus, we don't have to fear death or anything else. God's power has already won the victory, and we can live with the hope of eternal life. When we face forces that seem insurmountable, the key is to trust in God. Trusting God means believing that He is in control, even when we can't see how things will work out. Even when the path seems unclear or the problem feels too big, God's power can guide us and make a way. Knowing that God is in control gives us peace. When we bring our problems to God, He not only works in our situation but also gives us peace in our hearts. As believers, we are not powerless. God's power lives in us through the Holy Spirit. God's power isn't just something we see in the Bible—it's something we can experience in our own lives. When we rely on God's power, we can face anything with confidence. We don't have to be afraid of the future, worried about our problems, or overwhelmed by life's challenges. God's power is more than enough to carry us through.

Moving From Bondage To Freedom In God's Timing

Before we can understand how to move from bondage to freedom, we need to know what these two things mean. Bondage is anything that holds us down, keeps us from moving forward, or causes us to live in fear or guilt. It could be something like addiction, unforgiveness, or even a feeling of worthlessness. Freedom is the opposite—it's when we live with joy, peace, and hope, knowing we are no longer controlled by those negative things. Galatians 5:1 *"It is for freedom that Christ has set us free. Stand firm, then, and do not let yourselves be burdened again by a yoke of slavery."* God wants us to live in freedom, but we must trust Him and wait for His perfect timing. The first step in moving from bondage to freedom is recognizing what holds us back. Sometimes, we don't realize we're in bondage because we've gotten used to our situation. But God's Word helps us see the areas where we need change. John 8:34, *"Very truly I tell you, everyone who sins is a slave to sin."* Sin can trap us and lead us into bondage, but Jesus offers us the way out. Whether it's fear, anger, guilt, or anything else, we need to recognize these things and bring them to God. Moving from bondage to freedom doesn't always happen quickly. Sometimes, we may feel frustrated because we want freedom right away. But we must remember that God's timing is always perfect. God knows the right moment to set us free, and we can trust that He has a plan for us. His timing helps us grow and prepares us for the freedom He wants to give. It's important to have patience and trust that God is working in our lives, even when we can't see the changes immediately.

God doesn't just snap His fingers and make everything perfect right away. Moving from bondage to freedom often involves a process, and that process can be different for everyone. Sometimes, we are held in bondage by past pain, hurt, or disappointment. God wants to heal us, but healing takes time and requires us to be open to His help. If we're stuck in unhealthy patterns, like addiction or bad attitudes, God can help us break free, but it may take time and effort to change. Moving to freedom often means learning to trust God more deeply. As we learn to depend on Him, He helps us let go of the things that hold us back. Philippians 1:6, *"being confident of this, that he who began a good work in you will carry it on to completion until the day of Christ Jesus."* God doesn't give up on us, and He will continue working in our lives to bring us into freedom. There are times when God delivers us from difficult situations in a way that is quick and obvious. But there are also times when His deliverance is a process that takes longer. In the story of the Israelites in Exodus, God promised to deliver them from slavery in Egypt. However, He did not do it immediately. There were many trials and challenges along the way, but in the end, God led them to freedom. This reminds us that God's deliverance may take time, but we can trust that He is working behind the scenes. When we trust God and wait for His timing, He will give us the strength to keep going, even when we feel like giving up. Jesus came to earth to set us free from the power of sin. When we put our trust in Him, we can experience true freedom. This freedom allows us to live a life full of purpose, joy, and peace. Once God has brought us from bondage to freedom, we need to live in that freedom. This means making choices that align with God's will and not allowing ourselves to be trapped again by fear, sin, or the past. Romans 6:18, *"You have been set free from sin and have become slaves to righteousness."* Living in freedom means living in righteousness, following God's ways, and trusting that He will continue to guide us. As we experience the freedom God gives, we can also help others find freedom. Just as God set the Israelites free, He also wants us to share His message of freedom with others. 2 Corinthians 1:4, *"Who comforts us in all our troubles, so that we can comfort those in any trouble with the comfort we ourselves receive from God."* When we experience God's freedom, we can help others find that same freedom.

CHAPTER 3

BREAKTHROUGH IN THE FAMILY LINEAGE

Family lineage is the history or heritage of a family—what has been passed down from one generation to the next. This can include both good things and bad things. Sometimes, families pass down blessings, like wisdom, faith, and success. But other times, families may pass down struggles, like financial problems, health issues, or broken relationships. These struggles can feel like chains that hold the family down. A breakthrough happens when these negative patterns are broken, and God's power brings change. In the Bible, we see many examples of family lineages being affected by both blessings and curses. For example, Exodus 20:5, "You shall not bow down to them or worship them; for I, the Lord your God, am a jealous God, punishing the children for the sin of the parents to the third and fourth generation of those who hate me." This shows how the actions of parents can affect their children and grandchildren. However, the Bible also teaches that God's blessings can be passed down, and His grace can break generational curses. Generational curses are the negative patterns or struggles that get passed down through family lines. They could come from things like wrong choices, sinful habits, or spiritual bondage that the family faces. For example, if one generation struggles with addiction, that same problem may appear in the next generation. But the good news is that God has the power to break these curses. Through Jesus, we can be set free from any curse that has been passed down through our family. Jesus took the curse of sin and death on Himself, so that we can receive God's blessing instead. One of the first steps toward a family breakthrough is believing that God can change the family's history. God has the power to rewrite our family story, and He wants to bring healing and restoration to families. We need to trust that God can do the impossible, no matter what has happened in the past. Luke 1:37 "For no word from God will ever fail." This means that whatever God has promised, He will do. If God promises to bless your family and bring freedom from struggles, He will do it. All we need is faith to trust Him and believe that He is able to change things.

A breakthrough in the family often requires breaking the chains of bondage that have held the family back. These could be emotional chains, spiritual chains, or even physical chains like poverty or sickness. It's important to remember that God is a deliverer, and He has the power to break any chain. Isaiah 10:27, *"In that day their burden will be lifted from your shoulders, their yoke from your neck; the yoke will be broken because you have grown so fat."* When God brings breakthrough, He removes the burdens and chains that weigh us down. It's through His power that we are set free, and He can break the yokes of oppression in our family. One of the most powerful ways to invite breakthrough into our family is through prayer. Praying for the family lineage means asking God to break any negative cycles and to bless future generations. Prayer brings God's power into the situation and invites His transformation. When God brings breakthrough in the family, it is not just about breaking the bad patterns but also about restoring what has been lost. God wants to give us new beginnings, hope, and peace. In Joel 2:25 God promises, *"I will repay you for the years the locusts have eaten."* This means that God can restore what has been taken or damaged in the past, and He can give you something better in place of it. Through God's breakthrough, your family can experience healing in relationships, prosperity, good health, and peace. It is a fresh start, a new beginning where past mistakes and struggles are healed and replaced with God's goodness. One of the greatest outcomes of a family breakthrough is that it opens the door for blessings to be passed down to future generations. Once a family experiences freedom and restoration, those blessings don't just end with one person. They continue to flow to the children and grandchildren, creating a legacy of God's goodness.

Proverbs 20:7 *"The righteous who walks in his integrity—blessed are his children after him!"* A family that walks in God's ways can pass down blessings, faith, and wisdom to future generations. As God brings breakthrough in your family, you become part of a new legacy—one of victory, freedom, and faith.

Breaking Generational Curses And Claiming God's Promises

Generational curses refer to negative patterns, struggles, or behaviors that seem to be passed down from one generation to the next. These can include things like addiction, anger, poverty, or broken relationships. Sometimes, it feels like certain problems or struggles are just a part of a family's story, but the good news is that God offers us freedom from these cycles. Through faith, prayer, and claiming God's promises, we can break generational curses and start new, healthy patterns in our lives and the lives of our families. A generational curse happens when destructive habits or behaviors repeat over generations. For example, a family might have a history of unhealthy relationships, financial struggles, or poor health. It's important to note that not everything difficult in a family is a curse, but when problems seem to follow the same pattern over many years, they can feel like a curse. God doesn't want us to live under these curses, and He has given us the power to break free from them. The first step in breaking generational curses is recognizing them. If there are repeated issues in your family—like health problems, addiction, financial struggles, or anger—it's important to bring these to

God in prayer. Recognizing these negative patterns gives us the awareness to know what we need to pray about and seek God's help for. The Bible in Galatians 3:13 that, *"Christ redeemed us from the curse of the law by becoming a curse for us."* This means that Jesus took on the curse of sin when He died on the cross. Through His sacrifice, He made it possible for us to be free from generational curses. Through faith in Jesus, we can break the hold that these curses have on us. Luke 10:19, *"I have given you authority to trample on snakes and scorpions and to overcome all the power of the enemy; nothing will harm you."* God has given us many promises in His Word, and we can claim these promises over our lives and families. As we pray and trust in God's power, we can begin to see these curses broken and replaced with God's blessings. Breaking generational curses means starting a new pattern for future generations. Deuteronomy 30:19-20 *"This day I call the heavens and the earth as witnesses against you that I have set before you life and death, blessings and curses. Now choose life, so that you and your children may live."* Choosing to follow God and trust in His promises means that we can pass on a legacy of faith, hope, and blessing to our children and grandchildren.

Family is one of the most important parts of our lives, and sometimes it's the hardest area to see change. Family members may struggle with broken relationships, misunderstandings, or emotional pain. But God's Word teaches us that faith in Him has the power to restore families. When we have faith in God, we believe that He can heal wounds and restore what has been broken. This includes emotional wounds, physical illnesses, or damaged relationships. Jeremiah 30:17, *"But I will restore you to health and heal your wounds, declares the Lord."* No matter what has happened in the past, God can restore health and bring peace to families. Forgiveness is a big part of restoration. Often, the struggles in families come from hurt feelings or misunderstandings. When we choose to forgive, it opens the door for healing. Forgiving those who have hurt us can be hard, but it's an important step toward family restoration. When we forgive, we break the cycle of pain and make room for God's healing power to work. Faith in God's power can bring peace to our relationships. Trusting in God brings peace to our hearts, and that peace can spread to our families. Faith in God helps us to respond with love and understanding, even in difficult situations. One of the most powerful ways to bring restoration to your family is through prayer. Prayer connects us to God, and when we pray for our family, we invite God's presence and power into our homes. We can pray for healing, peace, and unity in our families. Prayer can help us see the changes that God is making, even when we don't immediately see the results. Once we have faith and pray for restoration, we must also take steps to live out that restoration. This means changing our behavior, loving one another, and living in a way that reflects God's love and peace. Living out restoration also means setting healthy boundaries, speaking kindly, and showing grace to one another. As we walk in faith and obedience, we will see God's restoration come to life in our families.

Understanding How God Transforms Family Dynamics

Families are the foundation of society. They are where we learn our first lessons about love, respect, and relationships. But like everything else in life, families can face challenges. Sometimes, there is conflict, miscommunication, or a lack of understanding. But the good news is that God wants to be involved in our families, and He can transform family dynamics—changing the way we relate to each other and helping us build stronger, healthier relationships. From the very beginning, God designed the family to be a place of love, support, and unity. Genesis 2:18 *"It is not good for the man to be alone. I will make a helper suitable for him."* God created the first family when He made Adam and Eve. The family was meant to reflect His love and care for His people. The Bible shows us that family is important to God, and He has specific plans for how families should operate. Ephesians 5:25 gives us an important instruction for husbands, saying, *"Husbands, love your wives, just as Christ loved the church and gave himself up for her."* This shows that God's design for marriage is built on sacrificial love and respect. Parents are also called to teach and guide their children in the ways of the Lord. Deuteronomy 6:7 says, *"Impress them on your children. Talk about them when you sit at home and when you walk along the road, when you lie down and when you get up."* God wants families to be a place where His love and teachings are passed down. One of the most powerful tools God gives us is prayer. When we pray for our families, we invite God to be a part of our relationships and situations. Prayer helps us communicate with God, seek His guidance, and ask for His help in changing hearts and minds. Through prayer, we can bring our worries and struggles before God, trusting that He will bring peace and healing. When we pray for our families, we can ask God to help us forgive one another, improve our communication, and help us grow in love. God hears our prayers, and He responds in His timing, often bringing healing and transformation to areas of our family life that need attention. The Bible teaches us to love one another as God loves us. This is a key part of how God transforms family dynamics. Love is the foundation of healthy family relationships 1 Corinthians 13:4-7. When family members love each other in this way, it changes everything. No matter what challenges come, love helps to heal wounds and build stronger bonds. If there is conflict in a family, learning to love with patience and kindness can bring understanding and reconciliation. When parents model God's love for their children, it creates an atmosphere of respect and trust.

Families are made up of imperfect people, and sometimes there is hurt, disappointment, or betrayal. These things can create division in a family. But God wants to heal these wounds and restore relationships. One of the key ways God transforms family dynamics is through the power of forgiveness. Forgiveness is not easy, but it is necessary for healing. When we forgive, we release the anger or bitterness that can divide us and create space for God's healing. When we practice forgiveness, it reflects God's grace toward us and helps to restore broken relationships in the family. Conflict is a natural part of family life, but how we handle it makes all the difference. God wants to help us navigate conflict in a healthy way, bringing peace and resolution. Matthew 18:15-17, *"If your brother or sister sins, go and point out their fault, just between the two of you. If they listen to you, you have won them over."* When there is conflict, God calls us to address it directly, with humility, and in love. Through the guidance of the Holy Spirit, we can learn to listen to one another, seek understanding, and find peaceful solutions. God can help us stop the cycle of fighting and bring peace to our homes. In God's design, children have an important role in the family. They are a blessing from God and are called to honor and obey their parents. Ephesians 6:1-3 *"Children, obey your parents in the Lord, for this is right. Honor your father and mother—which is the first commandment with a promise—so that it may go well with you and that you may enjoy long life on the earth."* When children obey and respect their parents, it creates harmony in the home. It also allows God to bless them and guide them. As children grow and develop, God also transforms their hearts, teaching them to love and serve others. Parents are called to raise their children in the ways of the Lord, teaching them about God's love and wisdom. A transformed family is one where unity and peace reign. God calls us to be peacemakers and to work toward unity in our families. Psalm 133:1 *"How good and pleasant it is when God's people live together in unity!"* Unity in the family brings joy, strength, and stability. When family members are united in love and purpose, they can face life's challenges together, knowing that they are supported and cared for. God wants to use transformed families to impact the world. When a family lives according to God's design, it becomes a witness to others. A family that is filled with love, forgiveness, peace, and unity becomes a reflection of God's kingdom here on earth. As families follow God's ways, they can become a powerful force for good in their communities and beyond.

CHAPTER 4

TRUSTING GOD'S PLAN FOR THE IMPOSSIBLE

Life can sometimes feel overwhelming, like we are facing challenges that are too big to overcome. There are moments when we may wonder how things will ever work out, especially when the problems seem impossible to solve. But in those very moments, God calls us to trust in His plan, even when we cannot see the way forward. God is not asking us to have perfect or huge faith; He just wants us to trust Him, even if our faith is small. This doesn't mean that we should have faith in our own abilities or in the things we can see. Instead, it means we trust in God's ability to do the impossible. When we focus on God and His power, rather than our problems, we allow Him to work in ways we cannot imagine. When we face tough situations, it's easy to focus on how big the problem is. We might feel like there's no way out or no solution in sight. God's plan is always bigger than any problem we face. Isaiah 55:8-9"For my thoughts are not your thoughts, neither are your ways my ways. As the heavens are higher than the earth, so are my ways higher than your ways and my thoughts than your thoughts." God sees the bigger picture, and He knows what's best for us. Even when we don't understand why things are happening, we can trust that God has a plan that is far greater than what we can see. There will be times when the challenges we face feel truly impossible. You may be dealing with health problems, financial struggles, broken relationships, or fears about the future. These situations can make us feel powerless. But God wants us to know that nothing is impossible for Him. Luke 1:37, "For no word from God will ever fail." This means that when God promises something, He will always make it happen, no matter how impossible it may seem. God is all-powerful, and He can do things that we cannot even begin to understand. When we trust in His power and His plan, we can face the impossible with hope.

Prayer is one of the most important ways we can trust God with our impossible situations. Through prayer, we talk to God, share our struggles, and ask for His help. God listens to our prayers and responds with love, wisdom, and guidance. Philippians 4:6-7, *"Do not be anxious about anything, but in every situation, by prayer and petition, with thanksgiving, present your requests to God. And the peace of God, which transcends all understanding, will guard your hearts and your minds in Christ Jesus."* When we pray, God gives us peace, even in the midst of challenges. We may not always get the answers we expect, but we can trust that God's plans are always for our good. Another important part of trusting God's plan is understanding that His timing is always perfect. Sometimes, we want things to change immediately, but God knows the right time for everything. Ecclesiastes 3:11 *"He has made everything beautiful in its time."* We might not see the beauty in our situation right away, but God is working behind the scenes. Trusting in God means waiting patiently for His perfect timing. God has given us many promises in the Bible, and we can trust that He will always keep His word. Even when life doesn't go as we expect, God is working for our good. His plan may look different from our own, but it is always better. God's plans are filled with hope, even when our situation seems hopeless, Jeremiah 29:11. Trusting God with the impossible requires action. Faith is not just something we feel; it's something we do. When we trust God, we also take steps of faith, knowing that He will guide us along the way. It might not be easy, and the path might not always be clear, but we can move forward, trusting that God will lead us. Even if we don't know what the future holds, we can have confidence that God is in control. We can step out in faith, trusting that God will provide what we need, open the doors that need to be opened, and close the ones that are not part of His plan. Living a life of trust in God means constantly relying on His strength, wisdom, and love. It means choosing to believe that God can do the impossible, even when we can't see how. Trusting God doesn't mean life will always be easy, but it means that no matter what happens, we know God is with us. Trusting God means surrendering our own understanding and relying fully on Him. When we do this, God guides our steps and makes a way for us, even through the impossible.

Moving Mountains And Transforming Nations With God's Power

God's power is unlimited and beyond our imagination. When we trust in Him, we can experience His incredible strength in our lives. One of the things God promises us is that with His power, we can do things that seem impossible. This includes moving mountains and transforming entire nations. The phrase "moving mountains" is often used to describe accomplishing something that seems impossible. Mountains are big, strong, and immovable. In the same way, there are situations in our lives that feel like giant obstacles—things we think we cannot change. However, Jesus teaches us that with God, nothing is impossible.

In Matthew 17:20, Jesus says, *"If you have faith as small as a mustard seed, you can say to this mountain, 'Move from here to there,' and it will move. Nothing will be impossible for you."* This doesn't mean that we literally move mountains, but it shows that with faith, God can help us overcome the biggest challenges in our lives. Mountains represent all the obstacles we face—whether it's personal struggles, problems in relationships, or even challenges in our communities. The key to moving mountains in our lives is faith. Faith means trusting in God, believing that He has the power to do anything, and knowing that He is with us through every challenge. It's not about having perfect faith, but even a small amount of faith can unlock the power of God. Mark 11:22-23, *"Have faith in God. Truly I tell you, if anyone says to this mountain, 'Go, throw yourself into the sea,' and does not doubt in their heart but believes that what they say will happen, it will be done for them."* This teaches us that if we truly trust God, we can see amazing things happen. When we face challenges, we can speak to them in faith and trust that God will work things out in His time. It's not just about our own strength, but about the power of God that works through us. Ephesians 3:20 *"Now to him who is able to do immeasurably more than all we ask or imagine, according to his power that is at work within us."* This means that God's power is in us and through us. When we face challenges, it is not by our own strength that we can overcome them, but by God's power working in us. This power can also help us bring change to the world around us. When we trust God and allow His power to work through us, we can become instruments of change, not just in our lives, but in our communities, cities, and even nations.

When we talk about transforming nations, we are talking about changing the hearts and lives of people in entire countries. This can sound overwhelming, but God is bigger than any problem or situation. He has the power to change nations, and He can use us as His instruments to bring that transformation. Matthew 28:19-20 Jesus gives us a mission to go into the world and make disciples of all nations: *"Therefore go and make disciples of all nations, baptizing them in the name of the Father and of the Son and of the Holy Spirit, and teaching them to obey everything I have commanded you."* This mission is not just for a few people; it's for all believers. As we share God's love and truth with others, we can see hearts changed, communities transformed, and nations impacted by His power. When God's people come together to pray, believe, and act in faith, we can see entire nations shift. The Bible is full of examples where God used just a few people to bring about major changes. For example, when the Israelites were in captivity, God used leaders like Moses to lead them to freedom and deliver them from oppression. Prayer is one of the most powerful ways we can partner with God to move mountains and bring change to nations. When we pray, we are asking God to intervene in our situations and in the world. Prayer connects us to God's power and allows Him to work in ways we can't always see. James 5:16 *"The prayer of a righteous person is powerful and effective."* Our prayers matter. When we pray for personal struggles, for our families, and for our nations, God hears us. He answers according to His will and in His perfect timing. If we believe that God can move mountains, we will see His power at work. We can pray for the leaders of nations, asking God to give them wisdom and guidance. We can pray for healing in nations suffering from war, poverty, and injustice. As believers, we can pray for the spread of the gospel to reach every part of the world, bringing hope and transformation to the hearts of people everywhere. God has a purpose for each of us, and that purpose is not just for our own benefit but to impact the world. God's plans for us are big and beyond our understanding. As we walk in His purpose, we are part of His bigger plan to bring His Kingdom to earth. This means we are called to be ambassadors of Christ, sharing His love, truth, and salvation with others. When we live out God's purpose, we can make a difference in the lives of individuals, families, communities, and nations. Through our actions, words, and prayers, we can see transformation take place. While we know that God has the power to move mountains and transform nations, we must understand that the road to transformation is not always easy. There will be challenges, opposition, and times when it seems like nothing is changing. But this is where faith and perseverance come in. Romans 8:37 *"No, in all these things we are more than conquerors through him who loved us."* We can be confident that no matter how hard the journey may seem, we are already victorious in Christ. With His power, we can overcome any challenge and see mountains move. As we continue to walk in faith, pray, and trust in God's power, we will begin to see change happen. It might not always be immediate, but God is always working behind the scenes. When we look back, we will see the impact of our prayers, actions, and faith in the lives of individuals and nations. In Isaiah 55:11 God promises that His Word will not return empty but will accomplish what He desires. *"So is my word that goes out from my mouth: It will not return to me empty, but will accomplish what I desire and achieve the purpose for which I sent it."* When we speak God's Word and walk in His power, we are participating in His plan to transform the world.

PART 2

RECONNECTING WITH GOD'S VOICE AND SPIRITUAL AUTHORITY

"God speaks in the language of the heart. We must tune our hearts to hear His voice." – Dallas Willard (from Hearing God: Developing a Conversational Relationship with God)

"My sheep listen to my voice; I know them, and they follow me." John 10:27 (NIV)

CHAPTER 5

RESTORING THE VOICE OF GOD IN YOUR LIFE

Saul was the first king of Israel, chosen by God to lead His people. When Saul began his reign, he started with good intentions, but over time, he allowed pride and disobedience to take root in his heart. The turning point came when Saul disobeyed God's command during a battle. In 1 Samuel 15:1-3 God gave Saul a clear command through the prophet Samuel: "Go and completely destroy the Amalekites, men, women, children, and animals... Do not spare them; put to death men and women, children and infants, cattle and sheep, camels and donkeys." This was a direct command from God to Saul, but Saul did not fully obey. He spared King Agag of the Amalekites and kept some of the best livestock for himself and his army, instead of destroying everything as God instructed. When Samuel confronted Saul about his disobedience, Saul tried to justify his actions by saying that he saved the animals to sacrifice to God (1 Samuel 15:20-21). But Samuel replied in 1 Samuel 15:22 "Does the Lord delight in burnt offerings and sacrifices as much as in obeying the Lord? To obey is better than sacrifice, and to heed is better than the fat of rams." Saul's disobedience showed that he valued his own plans over God's will. Because of Saul's disobedience, God rejected him as king. In 1 Samuel 15:23 Samuel told Saul: "For rebellion is like the sin of divination, and arrogance like the evil of idolatry." God was very clear: Saul's actions were not just mistakes but were rebellion against God's authority. As a result of Saul's rebellion, the relationship between Saul and God began to break down. God stopped speaking to Saul through the prophet Samuel. The Bible says that God withdrew His presence and stopped guiding Saul (1 Samuel 15:35). The voice of God became silent in Saul's life, and Saul could no longer hear God's direction. This is the tragic consequence of disobedience: God's voice can be silenced in our lives when we choose our own ways over His.

Saul's life shows us what happens when we turn away from God's voice. It's not that God is unwilling to speak to us; it's that our disobedience creates a barrier between us and Him. When we sin or ignore God's commands, it becomes harder to hear His voice clearly. The Bible teaches us that sin separates us from God. In Isaiah 59:2 *"But your iniquities have separated you from your God; your sins have hidden his face from you, so that he will not hear."* This means that when we live in disobedience, it blocks our ability to hear God clearly. Saul's life demonstrates this. After his rebellion, Saul desperately wanted God's guidance, but he could not hear God's voice anymore. In 1 Samuel 28:6 *"He inquired of the Lord, but the Lord did not answer him by dreams or Urim or prophets."* Saul was in a desperate situation, but because of his past disobedience, God remained silent. The good news is that God is always ready to restore His voice in our lives when we return to Him in repentance and obedience. If you feel that God's voice is silent in your life. The first step in restoring God's voice is to repent—turn away from any sin or disobedience in your life. Repentance means acknowledging that you have gone against God's will and asking for forgiveness. In 1 John 1:9 *"If we confess our sins, he is faithful and just and will forgive us our sins and purify us from all unrighteousness."* When we repent, God is faithful to forgive and restore us. God's voice is often found in His Word—the Bible. If we want to hear God's voice clearly, we need to obey what He has already spoken to us. John 14:23, *"Anyone who loves me will obey my teaching."* When we obey God's commands, we open the door for more of His guidance and direction in our lives. Just like Saul sought guidance from God through Samuel, we too must seek God through prayer. Prayer is our direct communication with God. James 4:8 *"Come near to God and he will come near to you."* When we spend time in prayer, we are making space for God to speak to us. It may take time, but as we continue seeking God, we will begin to hear His voice more clearly. Humility is essential to hearing God's voice. Saul's pride and arrogance led him to disobey God's commands, and that kept him from hearing God. In James 4:6 *"God opposes the proud but shows favor to the humble."* When we approach God with a humble heart, ready to listen and obey, He will speak to us. Sometimes, we may feel that God is silent simply because He is waiting for the right moment to speak. God speaks to us in His perfect timing. We must trust that He knows when we are ready to hear His voice and that His silence is often a part of His greater plan for us.

Recognizing When God Stops Speaking And How To Restore Communication

Communication with God is one of the most important aspects of a believer's life. Through prayer, reading the Bible, and listening to the Holy Spirit, God speaks to us, guiding us, comforting us, and helping us grow in our faith. However, there are times when it feels like God has stopped speaking or we don't hear from Him the way we used to. If this happens, it's important to understand why it happens and how we can restore that communication with God. Sometimes, when we don't hear God's voice, it can feel like He has stopped speaking. Our busy lives, filled with work, responsibilities, and personal issues, can cause us to lose focus on God. When we are too distracted, we may not hear Him clearly, even though He is still speaking to us. Jesus talks about this in Luke 8:14, where He says that the worries of life can choke the Word of God in our hearts. Sin can block our communication with God. When we live in sin and do not repent, it creates a barrier between us and God. Isaiah 59:2 says, *"But your iniquities have separated you from your God; your sins have hidden his face from you, so that he will not hear."* If we are living in disobedience, it can make it hard to hear God's voice. Sometimes, God may allow silence in our lives for a purpose. He might be testing our faith or teaching us to trust Him more. During times of silence, God may be drawing us closer to Him and teaching us how to listen to Him more deeply. When we don't make time for prayer or reading the Bible, we may find it harder to hear from God. The Bible is God's Word, and through it, He speaks to us. 2 Timothy 3:16-17 reminds us that all Scripture is God-breathed and useful for teaching, rebuking, correcting, and training in righteousness. Without spending time in God's Word, we might not recognize His voice as clearly.

It can sometimes be hard to recognize when God has stopped speaking because we may not be paying attention. God speaks peace into our hearts. When we are in tune with God, we feel peace, even in difficult situations. If you start feeling unrest or confusion in your spirit, it might be a sign that communication with God has been interrupted. If you feel spiritually dry or disconnected from God, it may indicate that communication has been cut off. It can feel like your prayers aren't being answered, or that reading the Bible no longer feels meaningful. This dryness can be a sign that something needs to change in your relationship with God. When God isn't speaking clearly, it may lead to doubts and confusion in your faith. If you are struggling to hear God's voice or understand His guidance, it might be a sign that something is blocking your communication with Him. When God feels distant, you may also feel isolated or alone in your spiritual journey. You might struggle to feel His presence or sense His guidance in your life. If you feel like God has stopped speaking, don't be discouraged. Communication can be restored. If sin is the reason for the silence, the first step to restoring communication is to repent. Confess your sins to God and ask for forgiveness. Repentance opens the door for God's voice to be heard again in our lives. If life's distractions have caused you to lose focus on God, it's time to make space for Him. Set aside time for quiet moments with God—whether it's through prayer, worship, or Bible study. Psalm 46:10, God to *"Be still, and know that I am God."* When we quiet our hearts, we make room for God's voice to be heard. Prayer is a two-way conversation. Sometimes, we focus too much on talking and not enough on listening. To restore communication, spend time listening to God in prayer. James 1:5 encourages us to ask God for wisdom, knowing He will give generously to all who ask. The Bible is where God speaks to us most clearly. Hebrews 4:12 says that the Word of God is alive and active, sharper than any double-edged sword. Make a habit of reading the Bible daily, asking God to speak to you through His Word. You can also meditate on verses and allow them to sink deep into your heart. There may be times when God allows silence to test our patience or strengthen our faith. Psalm 27:14, *"Wait for the Lord; be strong and take heart and wait for the Lord."* Trust that even in silence, God is working in your life. He may be preparing you for something greater, and waiting on Him can help us grow in faith and dependence on Him. Even when you can't hear God clearly, continue to worship and praise Him. Worship is an expression of trust, even when we don't understand what's happening. Psalm 34:1, *"I will bless the Lord at all times; his praise shall continually be in my mouth."* Worship can help restore your connection to God and remind you of His goodness and faithfulness. Sometimes, talking with trusted Christian friends or mentors can help you hear God's voice more clearly. They can pray with you and offer wisdom that may help you get back on track. Proverbs 11:14, *"For lack of guidance, a nation falls, but victory is won through many advisers."* Don't be afraid to seek counsel and prayer from others. Even when it feels like God is silent, remember that He is always present with you. Deuteronomy 31:6, *"Be strong and courageous. Do not be afraid or terrified because of them, for the Lord your God goes with you; he will never leave you nor forsake you."* God's silence does not mean His absence. He is always with us, even when we can't hear Him.

CHAPTER 6

THE POWER OF SPIRITUAL VISION AND INTERVENTION

Spiritual vision is the ability to see things from God's perspective. It's not about physical sight, but about seeing the truth in the spiritual world. God wants us to understand His plans, to see what He is doing in our lives, and to recognize how He is working around us. When we have spiritual vision, we can make decisions based on God's will, rather than being influenced only by what we see or feel in the natural world. Proverbs 29:18 (KJV), "Where there is no vision, the people perish." This means that without God's vision, we can easily lose our way and not know what God wants us to do. Spiritual vision helps us to see the path ahead and understand how God is guiding us. It is like a light in the darkness that shows us where to go. God desires to give us spiritual vision. He wants us to see what He is doing, not just what is happening around us. James 1:5 "If any of you lacks wisdom, let him ask of God, who gives to all liberally and without reproach, and it will be given to him." This means that when we ask God for guidance, He will give us the wisdom and understanding we need to see things as He sees them.

Spiritual vision also helps us see the battles we face in the spiritual realm. 2 Corinthians 4:18 *"So we fix our eyes not on what is seen, but on what is unseen, since what is seen is temporary, but what is unseen is eternal."* God's vision helps us look past the challenges we see in front of us and focus on the eternal promises He has for us. One of the most powerful ways that God works in our lives is through prayer. Prayer connects us to God's power and brings healing and deliverance. Jeremiah 33:3 *"Call to me and I will answer you and tell you great and unsearchable things you do not know."* Prayer is our way of reaching out to God, asking for His help, and believing that He will answer us. When we pray with faith, God moves powerfully in our lives. Healing is a powerful form of intervention that God offers. It can be physical, emotional, or spiritual. When we pray for healing, we are inviting God's power to touch every area of our lives and restore us to wholeness. Deliverance is another important form of intervention that happens through prayer. Deliverance refers to being set free from anything that holds us captive, whether it's sin, fear, addiction, or spiritual oppression. God's power is greater than any bondage we may face, and through prayer, we can be delivered. Luke 4:18, *"The Spirit of the Lord is on me, because he has anointed me to proclaim good news to the poor. He has sent me to proclaim freedom for the prisoners and recovery of sight for the blind, to set the oppressed free."* Jesus came to set us free, and through prayer, we can experience His freedom.

Prayer not only brings healing and deliverance but also intervenes in spiritual battles. We live in a world where there are spiritual forces at work—both good and evil. When we pray, we are engaging in a spiritual battle and asking God to fight for us. Ephesians 6:12 *"For our struggle is not against flesh and blood, but against the rulers, against the authorities, against the powers of this dark world and against the spiritual forces of evil in the heavenly realms."* This reminds us that our challenges are not just physical; they are spiritual too.

Prayer becomes our weapon in these battles. As we pray, we call on God to intervene and fight on our behalf. 2 Corinthians 10:4 *"The weapons we fight with are not the weapons of the world. On the contrary, they have divine power to demolish strongholds."*

Our prayers are powerful, and they can break down the spiritual strongholds that hold us back. Faith is a key part of receiving healing and deliverance through prayer. We must believe that God can do what He promises and trust that He will answer our prayers. In Mark 11:24, *"Therefore I tell you, whatever you ask for in prayer, believe that you have received it, and it will be yours."* When we pray with faith, we are trusting in God's power to heal and deliver us from all things.

Sometimes, healing and deliverance take time, and we may not see the results right away. However, we must continue to pray and trust God's timing. God's healing is not just physical; it also touches our emotions and spirits. We may face deep hurts from the past, disappointments, or struggles with sin. When we come to God in prayer, He wants to heal every part of us—body, mind, and spirit. Psalm 147:3 *"He heals the brokenhearted and binds up their wounds."* God is near to us in our pain and wants to bring healing to our hearts. Deliverance also includes freedom from past hurts, fears, and negative thoughts. As we pray, God can heal us from the inside out, setting us free from the things that hold us back. John 8:36 *"So if the Son sets you free, you will be free indeed."* Jesus offers complete freedom, and through prayer, we can experience that freedom in every area of our lives.

How God's Power Works Through Believers In Times Of Crisis

Life is full of unexpected challenges and moments of crisis. Sometimes, we face situations that feel overwhelming, and it can seem like there is no way out. One of the most comforting truths for believers is that God is always with us, especially in times of crisis. When we face difficulties, it might feel like we are alone, but God promises to never leave us. Psalm 46:1 *"God is our refuge and strength, an ever-present help in trouble."* This means that God is right there with us, ready to offer His help and support. His presence in our lives gives us the strength to face anything, knowing that we are not alone. In times of crisis, one of the greatest needs we have is peace. Stress, fear, and anxiety can overwhelm us, but God offers a peace that goes beyond understanding. God's peace is not like the peace the world offers. His peace comes from knowing that He is in control, even when everything around us seems out of control. When we trust God and pray to Him, His peace fills our hearts, helping us to remain calm in the midst of life's storms. When we face a crisis, we often feel weak and unable to handle the situation. But God's power works through our weakness. 2 Corinthians 12:9, *"My grace is sufficient for you, for my power is made perfect in weakness."* This means that when we feel weak, God's strength is shown in a greater way. Instead of relying on our own abilities, we can lean on God's strength, knowing that He can do far more than we can imagine.

When we feel weak, God can give us the courage to keep going, the wisdom to make decisions, and the endurance to face challenges. His power works best when we are humble enough to admit that we need His help. In our weakness, He makes us strong. When we pray, we are inviting God to step into our situation and work on our behalf. Prayer connects us to God's power and allows Him to intervene in our lives. Even when we don't know what to pray or how to pray, God hears us. The Holy Spirit helps us pray according to God's will, even when we can't find the words ourselves (Romans 8:26). Prayer brings us closer to God, and it opens the door for His power to work in our lives.

In times of crisis, God's Word provides us with strength, comfort, and guidance. The Bible is filled with promises that can help us stand firm when everything else seems uncertain. Psalm 119:105 *"Your word is a lamp for my feet, a light on my path."* When we are unsure of what to do or where to go, God's Word shows us the way. It reminds us of His faithfulness and His promises, giving us hope and strength to continue.

God's Word also teaches us how to respond in difficult situations. It reminds us to trust in God, to forgive, to love, and to endure. By reading and meditating on Scripture, we can find peace and wisdom in the middle of a crisis. God's power is not just at work in individual believers; it is also at work through the church, or the body of Christ. In times of crisis, the support of fellow believers can be a powerful reminder of God's love and care. 1 Corinthians 12:25-26 *"There should be no division in the body, but that its parts should have equal concern for each other. If one part suffers, every part suffers with it; if one part is honored, every part rejoices with it."* When we face struggles, God uses other believers to encourage, pray for, and support us. The body of Christ is meant to lift each other up, and through this support, God's power is made visible. Whether it's through a phone call, a prayer, or a helping hand, God's power works through His people to bring comfort and strength to those in crisis. While a crisis can feel overwhelming, God can use it for our growth and His greater purpose. Sometimes, God allows us to go through difficult times to refine our character and teach us to depend on Him more fully. Romans 5:3-4, *"Not only so, but we also glory in our sufferings, because we know that suffering produces perseverance; perseverance, character; and character, hope."*

God can use the trials we face to help us grow stronger in faith, develop patience, and build hope. While we may not understand the purpose of our struggles in the moment, we can trust that God is at work in us, using our pain to prepare us for something greater. In the end, we can look back and see how God used the crisis to shape us into the person He wants us to be. After a crisis, God is able to restore what has been lost or broken. Whether it's our peace, our relationships, or our sense of security, God is able to bring healing and restoration. Sometimes, a crisis leaves us feeling like we've lost so much, but God is faithful to restore and even make things better than before. He brings healing to our hearts, peace to our minds, and hope for the future. God's power works in our lives to bring victory over the crisis. No matter what the crisis is, God gives us the strength to overcome. Victory doesn't always look like we expect it, but God's victory in our lives means that we will come through the storm stronger, wiser, and more dependent on Him.

The Importance Of Spiritual Intervention And Acting In Obedience

Spiritual intervention is when God intervenes in our lives, stepping into our situations to help, guide, and bring about change. God, in His greatness, is always aware of our struggles, and He is ready to help when we turn to Him in prayer and faith. Sometimes, we cannot see a way out of a situation, but God can make a way where there seems to be no way. Isaiah 59:1, *"Surely the arm of the Lord is not too short to save, nor His ear too dull to hear."* This means that God's power is never limited, and He is always ready to hear our prayers and help us, no matter how impossible the situation may seem. Life is filled with challenges that we may not be able to solve on our own. Whether it's personal struggles, problems in our relationships, or difficult circumstances, we often reach a point where we need help. This is where spiritual intervention becomes essential. Sometimes, we don't even know what to ask for in prayer. But God knows our needs even before we ask. Matthew 6:8, *"Your Father knows what you need before you ask Him."* Spiritual intervention means trusting that God will provide what we need at the right time. We are limited in our abilities, but God is all-powerful. When we face situations beyond our control, God can step in and do what we cannot. For example, in Exodus 14:21-22 when the Israelites were trapped between the Red Sea and the Egyptian army, God parted the sea so they could escape. That was a miraculous act of spiritual intervention. God's intervention often comes in different ways, and we might not always understand how He works. But we can trust that He knows what is best for us. God's Holy Spirit is our helper and guide. John 14:26, *"But the Advocate, the Holy Spirit, whom the Father will send in my name, will teach you all things and will remind you of everything I have said to you."* The Holy Spirit helps us make decisions, gives us wisdom, and directs us in the right way. God often answers our prayers in ways that surprise us. When we pray and trust God, we open the door for

His intervention. Sometimes, God works in miraculous ways. He can heal, provide, or protect us in situations that seem impossible. Psalm 34:7 *"The angel of the Lord encamps around those who fear Him, and He delivers them."* God is always watching over us, and He sends His angels to protect us.

While spiritual intervention is all about God's action in our lives, we also have a role to play. Obedience is an important part of receiving God's intervention. When we obey God, we show that we trust Him, and He responds by guiding us and stepping into our situations. Our obedience shows God that we trust Him and want to follow His will. When we are obedient, God blesses us and works on our behalf. Deuteronomy 28:1-2 *"If you fully obey the Lord your God and carefully follow all His commands... all these blessings will come on you and accompany you if you obey the Lord your God."* Obeying God's commands brings His favor and allows His intervention to take place in our lives. Sometimes, God asks us to do things that don't make sense in the natural. But when we obey in faith, we make space for His power to work. Obedience is an expression of faith. It's easy to obey God when things are going well, but it's much harder when we are facing difficulties. However, obedience in tough times is one of the greatest ways we can experience God's intervention. Proverbs 3:5-6, *"Trust in the Lord with all your heart and lean not on your own understanding; in all your ways submit to Him, and He will make your paths straight."* Even when we don't understand what God is doing, we can trust that He knows what is best. Sometimes, God allows us to go through difficult times to strengthen our faith. Romans 5:3-4 *"Not only so, but we also glory in our sufferings, because we know that suffering produces perseverance; perseverance, character; and character, hope."* When we obey God in times of suffering, it strengthens our character and builds hope. When we choose to obey God, there are great rewards. Obedience brings peace, joy, and God's favor into our lives. It also allows us to experience God's presence and intervention in powerful ways. In Matthew 11:28-30 Jesus invites us, *"Come to me, all you who are weary and burdened, and I will give you rest."* Obedience to God brings rest to our hearts and minds, even in the middle of challenges. When we follow God's will, we experience true joy.

CHAPTER 7

BECOMING A FORCE IN THE SPIRITUAL REALM

The spiritual realm is a place that exists beyond what we can see with our eyes. It is where God's power and His angels are at work, and where we can connect with Him in prayer and worship. When we become Christians, we are not just living in this world—we are also part of a greater spiritual battle. But we don't have to fight this battle alone. Through prayer, worship, and faith, we can tap into the power of God and become active participants in the spiritual realm. One of the first steps in becoming a force in the spiritual realm is understanding that we have access to God's power. As believers, God has given us the Holy Spirit to guide us, empower us, and help us in our spiritual journey. Acts 1:8 , "But you will receive power when the Holy Spirit comes on you; and you will be my witnesses in Jerusalem, and in all Judea and Samaria, and to the ends of the earth." The Holy Spirit gives us power to do things that are beyond our natural abilities.

When we connect with God through prayer, worship, and reading the Bible, we are drawing closer to His power. The more we seek God, the more we are filled with His strength and ability to do things in the spiritual realm. Prayer is one of the most important ways we connect with the spiritual realm. Through prayer, we communicate with God and invite His power to work in our lives.

Prayer also allows us to be spiritually aware and sensitive to what God is doing in the world around us. it is a constant part of our lives that keeps us connected to God's power. Through prayer, we can spiritually transport ourselves to places of need. For example, if someone we know is in need of healing or deliverance, we can pray for them from wherever we are. We don't need to be physically present; our prayers have the power to reach them, because we are inviting
God's power into their situation. Faith is another key element in becoming a force in the spiritual realm. When we pray with faith, believing that God can do anything, we unlock His power.

To become a force in the spiritual realm, we need to be led by the Holy Spirit. The Holy Spirit is our guide and helper in this life. He helps us understand God's will, gives us wisdom, and empowers us to live out our calling. Being led by the Holy Spirit allows us to respond to the needs around us. Sometimes, the Spirit may prompt us to pray for someone or to speak into a situation, and when we obey, God's power is released. The Holy Spirit also helps us spiritually transport ourselves to the places of need. When we follow His guidance, He may lead us to pray for a situation in another country, or to intercede for someone who is far away. One of the powerful ways we can spiritually transport ourselves to places of need is through intercessory prayer. Intercession is when we pray on behalf of others, asking God to intervene in their lives. When we intercede, we are standing in the gap for someone else, asking God to bring healing, deliverance, or breakthrough in their situation. We can intercede for others, even when we are not physically present with them. Ezekiel 22:30 *"I looked for someone among them who would build up the wall and stand before me in the gap on behalf of the land..."* As intercessors, we stand in the gap, praying for God's intervention in the lives of others. This kind of prayer transcends distance and time, because God is not limited by geography. Through prayer, we can spiritually transport ourselves to any place of need and ask God to move. Another way to become a force in the spiritual realm is through spiritual warfare. Spiritual warfare involves using prayer and God's Word to fight against the powers of darkness that try to attack us and those around us. The Bible that we are in a spiritual battle, but we are not left defenseless. We have weapons of warfare that are powerful and effective.

Our spiritual weapons are powerful because they are backed by God's power. These weapons include prayer, the Word of God, and the authority we have as believers. When we use these weapons, we can overcome the enemy's attacks and bring freedom to people who are in bondage.

Through spiritual warfare, we can spiritually transport ourselves to places where the enemy is at work, whether it's in a person's life, a family, or even a nation. By praying and declaring God's victory over these situations, we can bring change and freedom. As believers, God has given us authority to act in His name. Luke 10:19, This means that we have authority over the enemy and his schemes. When we walk in this authority, we can pray with confidence and see God's power at work. Using our authority in Christ allows us to spiritually transport ourselves to places of need and bring God's power into those situations. Whether we are praying for healing, deliverance, or breakthrough, we can do so with the authority given to us by Jesus. To become a force in the spiritual realm, we must live with a kingdom mindset. This means we see the world through the lens of God's Kingdom, understanding that we are called to bring His will to earth. When we pray with this mindset, we are asking God to bring His Kingdom to earth, and we are willing to be used by Him to make that happen. A kingdom mindset allows us to see beyond our own lives and focus on what God wants to do in the world. It helps us understand that we are part of His bigger plan to bring change and transformation, and that we have the power to be part of that plan through prayer, faith, and action.

Becoming Spiritually Empowered To Confront And Overcome Adversity

Spiritual empowerment means receiving the strength, wisdom, and guidance from God to live a victorious life. It's not about relying on our own strength but depending on God's power to help us navigate the challenges we face. When we are spiritually empowered, we can approach adversity with a sense of peace and confidence, knowing that God is with us and will see us through. In Philippians 4:13 the Apostle Paul writes, *"I can do all this through him who gives me strength."* This verse reminds us that no matter how difficult the situation is, we have the strength to endure because of God's power in us. Spiritual empowerment is about tapping into that divine strength that comes from our relationship with God. One of the key components of spiritual empowerment is faith. Faith is the foundation that allows us to trust in God's promises, even when things don't make sense or when we can't see the outcome. It's easy to doubt when life is hard, but God calls us to trust Him, knowing that He is faithful and will never leave us. James 1:2-3 *"Consider it pure joy, my brothers and sisters, whenever you face trials of many kinds, because you know that the testing of your faith produces perseverance."* Trials and adversity are part of life, but they are also opportunities to grow in faith. When we trust God during difficult times, our faith becomes stronger, and we become more spiritually empowered to face future challenges. When we face adversity, it's natural to feel weak and overwhelmed. But in those moments, we must remember that God's strength is greater than our own. In Isaiah 40:29-31 God promises to give strength to the weary: *"He gives strength to the weary and increases the power of the weak. Even youths grow tired and weary, and young men stumble and fall; but those who hope in the Lord will renew their strength. They will soar on wings like eagles; they will run and not grow weary, they will walk and not be faint."* This passage reminds us that God will renew our strength when we feel exhausted. When we rely on His power, we can keep going even when it seems impossible. No matter how tired or defeated we may feel, God's strength is always available to lift us up and carry us through.

God has made many promises to His people in the Bible. When we face adversity, it's important to remind ourselves of these promises and hold on to them. God's promises give us hope and help us to stay strong, even when everything around us seems uncertain. No matter what happens, God is working behind the scenes for our good. Even in times of difficulty, He has a plan for us, and He is using our struggles to shape us into the people He wants us to be. Another promise is found in Deuteronomy 31:6 *"Be strong and courageous. Do not be afraid or terrified because of them, for the Lord your God goes with you; he will never leave you nor forsake you."* This reminds us that God is always with us. We can face any adversity with confidence because we know that God will never leave our side. Worship is not just something we do when things are going well; it's also an important way to stay spiritually empowered during tough times. Worship helps us shift our focus from our problems to God's greatness. When we worship, we declare that God is in control, and we acknowledge His power over every situation. In Acts 16:25-26 Paul and Silas were in prison, facing unfair treatment and suffering. But instead of complaining or feeling defeated, they prayed and sang hymns to God. As they worshiped, God sent an earthquake to free them from their chains. This story shows us that worship can bring breakthrough and deliverance, even in the darkest times. Adversity can be tough, but it's important to remember that God uses trials to build our character. When we face difficulties, we have the opportunity to persevere and grow stronger in our faith. Perseverance is key to overcoming adversity, and as we keep going, God continues to shape us into the people He wants us to be. God uses them to develop qualities like perseverance and character, which help us become more spiritually empowered. One of the hardest things about facing adversity is that we don't always understand why things happen or when they will end. However, God's timing is perfect, and He knows exactly when and how to bring us through our struggles. Trusting in His timing helps us remain patient and hopeful during difficult times. As spiritually empowered believers, we are called to walk in victory, no matter the circumstances. Jesus has already won the ultimate victory over sin, death, and all the powers of darkness. Through His victory, we have the assurance that we too can overcome any adversity that comes our way. Our faith in Jesus gives us victory. We are not defeated by our struggles; instead, we are more than conquerors through Christ.

Walking In Divine Authority For Spiritual Victory

As believers in Christ, we are given the amazing gift of divine authority. This means that God has given us the power to overcome spiritual battles, resist evil, and live a victorious life. Walking in this authority is not about being strong in ourselves, but about recognizing and relying on the strength and power that God has given us through Jesus Christ. Divine authority is the power that God has given to believers to rule and reign in the spiritual realm. It is not our own power, but God's power working in and through us. Through Jesus' death and resurrection, He defeated the enemy and gave us the authority to stand against anything that comes against us. Luke 10:19, *"I have given you authority to trample on snakes and scorpions and to overcome all the power of the enemy; nothing will harm you."* This verse shows that as believers, we are given authority over all the attacks of the enemy. We don't have to live in fear or defeat because God has already given us the power to overcome. When we accept Jesus as our Lord and Savior, we are given His authority. Jesus was given all authority in heaven and on earth, and because we are in Him, we share in that authority. Matthew 28:18, *"All authority in heaven and on earth has been given to me."* As His followers, we have the privilege of walking in that same authority. This means we can stand strong in the face of challenges, knowing that we are not alone. God has given us the power to win every spiritual battle we face. Spiritual victory is the success we experience when we walk in the authority that God has given us. It is not about our own efforts or strength, but about relying on God's power to overcome the challenges and attacks of the enemy. This victory is already won through Jesus, and we must walk in that victory daily. 1 Corinthians 15:57 *"But thanks be to God! He gives us the victory through our Lord Jesus Christ."* The victory is already ours, but we must choose to walk in it. Spiritual victory means living in the fullness of what Jesus has accomplished for us—freedom from sin, freedom from fear, and freedom from the power of the enemy.

Walking in divine authority is about trusting in God's power, knowing who we are in Christ, and standing firm in faith. Understanding who you are in Christ is key to walking in divine authority. As a believer, you are a child of God, and you have been made righteous in Christ. Romans 8:17 *"Now if we are children, then we are heirs—heirs of God and co-heirs with Christ."* This means that everything that belongs to Christ belongs to you as well. You have the authority to claim what is yours in Christ, including victory over sin, sickness, and the enemy. Faith is the key to activating the authority God has given you. Ephesians 6:16 *"In addition to all this, take up the shield of faith, with which you can extinguish all the flaming arrows of the evil one."* When you face challenges or spiritual attacks, you must stand firm in faith, knowing that God has already given you victory. God's Word is powerful. When we speak His Word, we release His authority over situations. Matthew 21:21-22, *"Truly I tell you, if you have faith and do not doubt, not only can you do what was done to the fig tree, but also you can say to this mountain, 'Go, throw yourself into the sea,' and it will be done."* Speaking God's Word over our situations brings His authority into action. Whether you are dealing with fear, sickness, or discouragement, speak the truth of God's Word and trust that His authority will bring victory. Prayer is one of the most powerful ways to walk in divine authority. When you pray, you are communicating with God and inviting His power into your life. When you pray with faith, you are exercising your authority in Christ. Pray boldly, knowing that God hears you and will answer according to His will. The enemy will try to attack you and cause fear, doubt, and confusion. However, God has given you the authority to resist him. James 4:7 *"Submit yourselves, then, to God. Resist the devil, and he will flee from you."* When you face spiritual battles, remember that you have the power to resist the enemy. You don't have to accept his lies or attacks. Stand firm in your authority and command him to leave.

Walking in divine authority is not just something we do in moments of crisis. It is a lifestyle. When you live every day in the awareness of God's authority, you begin to experience constant victory in your life. It's about living with the mindset that you are not a victim, but a victor in Christ. You are not just an overcomer—you are more than a conqueror. This means that you don't just win battles, but you live in the victory that Jesus has already won for you. The Holy Spirit plays a vital role in walking in divine authority. He empowers us, guides us, and strengthens us in our spiritual walk. The Holy Spirit is the source of our power to live victoriously and walk in divine authority. One of the most important aspects of walking in divine authority is knowing that you have victory over the enemy. Colossians 2:15 *"And having disarmed the powers and authorities, he made a public spectacle of them, triumphing over them by the cross."* Through Jesus' death on the cross, He defeated all powers of darkness. As a believer, you share in that victory. You don't have to be afraid of the enemy because Jesus has already overcome him.

PART 3

RISING ABOVE LIFE'S CHALLENGES

"Faith does not make things easy, it makes them possible."- Mark 9:23, as paraphrased by Max Lucado

"I can do all this through him who gives me strength."

This verse reminds us that with God's strength, we are able to rise above any challenge. Through His help, what seems impossible can become possible, and we can overcome life's toughest situations. Philippians 4:13 (NIV)

CHAPTER 8

CONQUERING THE CONTRADICTIONS OF YOUR PAST

We all have things in our past that we might not be proud of—mistakes, failures, or things that have hurt us. These experiences can often create contradictions in our lives, where we feel like we are not good enough or that we are not worthy of the good things God has for us. But just like David in the Bible, God has a plan to help us overcome our past and rise to the purpose He has for us. A contradiction is when two things seem to be opposite or don't make sense together. For example, you might feel like God has big plans for your life, but your past tells you that you are not capable or that you don't deserve success. These contradictions can cause confusion and even fear. However, it is important to remember that God's love and purpose for us are greater than any mistakes or struggles in our past.

David's life is a perfect example of overcoming contradictions. He was a young shepherd boy with little experience or status, yet God chose him to be a king. His story shows us that no matter what our past looks like, God can use us for something great. David didn't come from a royal family or have a prestigious background. In fact, he was the youngest of his brothers, and when the prophet

Samuel came to anoint the next king of Israel, David was not even considered important enough to be invited to the ceremony (1 Samuel 16:10-11). His family saw him as just a shepherd, someone who tended to sheep. But God saw his heart and knew that he was the one to lead Israel. No matter how humble or unimportant you may feel because of your past, God looks at your heart. He is not concerned with your background or your mistakes. What matters to God is your willingness to trust and obey Him. One of the most remarkable things about David was his heart. Despite his past, despite his mistakes, and even despite his failures, David was described as "a man after God's own heart" (Acts 13:22). What does that mean? It means that David sought God in all things. He trusted God and sought His guidance, even when facing great challenges.

David's heart was not perfect, but he was humble enough to repent when he sinned. In Psalm 51:10, David prayed, *"Create in me a pure heart, O God, and renew a steadfast spirit within me."* He was not afraid to admit his mistakes and ask for God's forgiveness. This is a key part of overcoming the contradictions in our past: acknowledging our failures, repenting, and allowing God to transform our hearts. You do not have to be perfect to be used by God. What matters is that your heart is turned toward Him, and that you are willing to grow and learn from your mistakes.

Even though David started out as a lowly shepherd, he eventually became king of Israel. His rise to prominence was not an easy or straightforward journey. Along the way, he faced many challenges —he had to fight Goliath, deal with the jealousy of King Saul, and hide in caves to escape from those who wanted to kill him. But through it all, David trusted God. He never let the contradictions of his past or the difficulties of his present stop him from moving forward in the purpose God had for him. One of the most powerful moments in David's life was when he faced Goliath, the giant. In 1 Samuel 17:45, David said to Goliath, *"You come against me with sword and spear, but I come against you in the name of the Lord Almighty..."* David did not rely on his own strength or abilities, but on God's power. This shows us that even when we face giants or seemingly impossible situations, we must rely on God to give us the strength to conquer them. Your past does not define your future. No matter where you start, if you trust in God and keep moving forward, He will open doors for you and help you rise to the place He has called you to. When we look at David's life, we see a man who had every reason to give up because of the contradictions in his life. From being an unnoticed shepherd to facing enemies who tried to kill him, David had many reasons to doubt God's plan for him. But he chose to trust in God, and through his faith, God brought him to a place of great prominence. In the same way, you can overcome the contradictions of your past. No matter what mistakes you've made or how others have treated you, God has a great plan for your life. He can turn your past into a testimony of His power and grace. God has a purpose for your life, and no matter where you come from or what you've been through, He can help you conquer the contradictions and move forward into the future He has for you. Part of conquering the contradictions of your past is allowing God to heal and restore you. David faced deep pain and loss in his life, including the loss of a child, betrayal by close friends, and the mistakes he made. But through it all, God was with him, healing his wounds and restoring his soul. In Psalm 23:3, David wrote, *"He refreshes my soul. He guides me along the right paths for his name's sake."* This shows that even in the darkest times, God is there to refresh and restore us. When we allow God to heal our brokenness, we can move beyond our past and step into the bright future He has for us. Let God heal the wounds of your past. You don't have to carry the weight of your mistakes or hurts. God wants to restore you and help you live out His plan for your life. David's journey to becoming king wasn't an overnight success. It took years of waiting, trusting, and overcoming obstacles. But he knew that God had a plan for his life. In the same way, God has a plan for you, and even when things don't make sense, you can trust that He is working behind the scenes to bring you into the place He has prepared for you. Trusting in God and His timing will help you conquer the contradictions of your past and lead you into your future.

Overcoming The Challenges And Contradictions In Your Family And Past

Family should be a place where we feel loved, supported, and encouraged. But in reality, not all families experience this kind of harmony. Sometimes, families face misunderstandings, arguments, or even deep hurts that linger for years. Challenges in families can stem from anger, neglect, abuse, or broken relationships that were never healed. These situations can make us feel trapped, hurt, or even hopeless.

It's essential to know that family challenges do not define who we are. The difficulties we face in our families don't mean that we are destined to carry the same pain or repeat the same mistakes. God has the power to heal our hearts and break the cycle of dysfunction. Isaiah 61:1, *"He has sent me to bind up the brokenhearted, to proclaim freedom for the captives and release from darkness for the prisoners."* God promise to heal our brokenness, set us free from the burdens of the past, and bring light into the darkest parts of our lives. No matter how complicated or painful our family situations may seem, God offers healing and restoration. Past hurts can deeply impact how we live today. The pain we experience in childhood or later in life can leave scars on our hearts and minds. These wounds might affect how we see ourselves, how we interact with others, and even how we trust God. But God doesn't want us to carry the weight of our past forever. He promises to heal us and make us new. 2 Corinthians 5:17, *"Therefore, if anyone is in Christ, the new creation has come: The old has gone, the new is here!"* When we come to Jesus, He gives us a fresh start. The struggles and pain from our past don't have to define us anymore. We can leave the old behind and step into the new life that God offers. One of the first steps to healing is forgiveness. Forgiveness doesn't mean that what happened was okay, but it's about letting go of the pain that holds us back.

Forgiving someone is a choice to release them to God and free ourselves from the burden of bitterness. Matthew 6:14-15,*"For if you forgive other people when they sin against you, your heavenly Father will also forgive you. But if you do not forgive others their sins, your Father will not forgive your sins."* Forgiveness is more about our own healing than about the person who hurt us. When we forgive, we allow God to bring peace into our hearts and help us move forward.

Healing is a process, and it may take time. It's okay to feel the pain, but we must bring it to God, trusting that He will gently restore us and make us whole again. In some families, negative patterns seem to repeat over generations. These cycles might include anger, addiction, fear, or unforgiveness. They can feel like chains, making it seem impossible to live differently. But with God, we can break these cycles and create a healthier, more loving future for ourselves and our families. God can renew our minds and transform our hearts, giving us the strength to break free from old habits and start fresh. Admit that something needs to change. Acknowledge the patterns of dysfunction in your family and bring them to God in prayer. Breaking free requires trusting God and allowing Him to lead. Ask Him to help you let go of old ways and guide you into new, healthier patterns. Spend time in God's Word and let His truth shape your thoughts and actions. Replace lies like "This is just how it is" with God's promises of hope and transformation. Sometimes, breaking the cycle means reaching out to trusted counselors, mentors, or church leaders for guidance and support. Healing often happens in community, where others can encourage and pray for you. Commit to making choices that reflect God's love and truth. This might involve setting boundaries, choosing forgiveness, and modeling healthy behaviors for your family. When we invite Jesus into our struggles, He breaks the chains that hold us back. He empowers us to live in freedom and to create a new story for ourselves and our families—a story of love, hope, and faith.

The enemy often tries to deceive us with lies about our worth and our future. He uses our past mistakes, family struggles, and insecurities to make us feel unworthy, hopeless, and stuck. He whispers things like, *"You'll never be good enough,"* or *"You're just like your parents—you'll never change."* These lies can keep us trapped in fear and pain, unable to move forward.

But here's the good news: these lies are not the truth. God's Word tells us what is true, and it is the truth that sets us free. John 8:32, *"Then you will know the truth, and the truth will set you free."* The truth is that God loves us, and He has a good plan for our lives. He doesn't see us through the lens of our past. Instead, through Jesus, we are made new and empowered to live a life of purpose and victory. When we hear the enemy's lies, we can fight back with God's truth. Speak His promises out loud. For example, when the enemy says, *"You're not enough,"* declare Philippians 4:13, Romans 8:37. God's truth reminds us that we are not victims of our past —we are victors in Christ. As we overcome the lies of the enemy, we can begin to heal from our past and focus on building stronger family relationships. Healing takes time, but with God's help, we can move toward restoration and unity. This process requires three key things: patience, forgiveness, and understanding. Building stronger relationships means showing kindness and forgiveness, even when it's hard. When we forgive, we reflect God's love, and we open the door for healing in our families. Even when family struggles and past challenges feel overwhelming, we can trust God to restore what has been broken. God is a restorer, and He can heal relationships, rebuild trust, and renew our hearts. No matter what has been lost—time, joy, or connection—God can give us back more than we thought possible. Restoration doesn't always happen overnight, but it begins when we trust God and believe that He is working behind the scenes. Here's how you can trust God for restoration: Once we experience healing and restoration, it's important to move forward in faith. The past may have been painful, but it doesn't have to define our future. Philippians 3:13-14, *"Forgetting what is behind and straining toward what is ahead, I press on toward the goal to win the prize for which God has called me heavenward in Christ Jesus."* Moving forward means letting go of old hurts, mistakes, and disappointments. It means choosing to trust God with the future and walking in the hope He gives. God's plan for your life is greater than your past. As you move forward, He will equip you to live in freedom, love, and purpose. He will use your testimony to inspire others and bring glory to His name. Remember, you are not alone—God is with you every step of the way.

How God Uses The Broken Pieces For His Glory

Life often brings pain, disappointment, and struggles. We can feel broken—like pieces of our heart, dreams, or hopes have been shattered. Whether it's through loss, failure, betrayal, or personal weaknesses, it's easy to think that our brokenness disqualifies us or that God can't use us. But the truth is, God specializes in taking broken things and making them beautiful. He uses our broken pieces for His glory in ways we might not understand. When we experience brokenness, we may feel worthless or hopeless. However, God sees our pain differently. He sees the potential in us, even in our brokenness. Just like a potter who shapes clay into something beautiful, God takes the broken pieces of our lives and molds them into something special. Isaiah 64:8 *"Yet you, Lord, are our Father. We are the clay, you are the potter; we are all the work of your hand."* This verse reminds us that God is the master potter. He is at work in our lives, even when we don't see it. Our brokenness doesn't scare Him—it's an opportunity for Him to work more deeply in us and create something new. Sometimes, God allows us to experience brokenness to bring us closer to Him. When everything else seems to fall apart, we can find comfort and strength in His presence. Our brokenness makes us realize that we need God. It's through our weaknesses that we experience His strength. In our weakness, God's power shines brightest. When we are broken, we are more open to depending on God and trusting in His grace. Sometimes, before God can heal us, He needs to break us. Just like a broken bone needs to be set in place to heal properly, our hearts need to be broken before they can be truly healed. God doesn't break us to hurt us, but to heal us in a deeper way. Psalm 34:18 *"The Lord is close to the brokenhearted and saves those who are crushed in spirit."* God is near to us when we are broken and hurting. He doesn't leave us in our brokenness; He works in us and through us to bring healing. When we are broken, it often leads to humility. We realize that we are not in control and that we need God more than ever. Brokenness can teach us to depend on Him, not on our own strength or abilities. James 4:10 *"Humble yourselves before the Lord, and he will lift you up."* God allows brokenness to teach us humility so that we can grow closer to Him. Humility opens our hearts to receive God's healing and guidance.

One of the most amazing things about God is how He can take something broken and make it whole again. Our brokenness becomes a place where God's power is displayed. When we are at our lowest, God shows up with His strength and power. In 2 Corinthians 4:7 Paul says, *"But we have this treasure in jars of clay to show that this all-surpassing power is from God and not from us."* God uses broken people to display His incredible power. Our brokenness becomes a testimony of His grace and strength. When we go through difficult times, it's easy to feel alone, but God often uses our brokenness to help others who are going through similar struggles. When God heals us, He can use our story to bring hope to others. God allows us to go through pain and brokenness so that we can comfort others in their pain. When we share how God healed us, others can find hope in Him. When God restores us from brokenness, it brings glory to Him. Our restoration shows the world that God is powerful and loving. It's a testimony of His ability to heal and restore, even when things seem impossible. The ultimate example of God using brokenness for His glory is found in the life of Jesus. Jesus was broken for us on the cross. His body was physically broken, but through His brokenness, He brought salvation to the world. Isaiah 53:5 *"But he was pierced for our transgressions, he was crushed for our iniquities; the punishment that brought us peace was on him, and by his wounds we are healed."* Jesus' brokenness was not in vain. It was used to bring healing, forgiveness, and freedom to all of humanity. Through His brokenness, God displayed the greatest act of love and victory. God doesn't waste anything, even our pain. He uses every part of our story, including the broken parts, to fulfill His purpose. God's plan is not to leave us broken, but to restore and use us for His glory. As we surrender our brokenness to Him, He works in us and through us to bring about His plans. Even in our brokenness, God is at work. He uses everything for good and will bring healing, growth, and restoration into our lives.

CHAPTER 9

THE BATTLE FOR YOUR DESTINY

In life, every person faces challenges, obstacles, and battles that threaten to stop us from reaching our true potential. But just as David faced the giant Goliath, each of us has the opportunity to overcome the battles in our lives. Our destiny is shaped by how we respond to the challenges that come our way. David's story teaches us that it's not about how big the challenges are, but about the strength and faith we have in God to face them. Your destiny is the plan and purpose that God has for your life. It's the reason you were created and the path He wants you to walk. However, the road to fulfilling your destiny is not always easy. Just like David had to fight against Goliath, we often face difficulties that can seem too big to overcome. These challenges can be things like fear, doubt, insecurities, or even external obstacles that try to stop us from becoming who God wants us to be. The battle for your destiny is not a physical fight, but a spiritual one. It's a fight between the life God has for you and the things that try to hold you back. This could be negative thoughts, the enemy's attacks, or the obstacles that life throws your way. However, like David, you can overcome these challenges with the right heart, faith, and trust in God. David was just a young shepherd when he faced Goliath, a giant warrior who terrified the whole army of Israel. David wasn't afraid of Goliath because he had something that others didn't—a heart full of faith and trust in God. David's heart was different because he knew that God was bigger than any problem, any giant, or any enemy. David had already experienced God's faithfulness when protecting his sheep from lions and bears, so he trusted that God would protect him against Goliath as well. 1 Samuel 17:37, "The Lord who rescued me from the paw of the lion and the paw of the bear will rescue me from the hand of this Philistine." David's heart was filled with faith in the power of God, and that faith made all the difference. David's victory over Goliath didn't come from his size or strength, but from his heart. The battle for your destiny starts in your heart. If you allow fear, doubt, or negative thoughts to control your heart, they will defeat you. But if you have a heart of faith, courage, and trust in God, you will be able to face any challenge. God sees our hearts, and it is through our hearts that He empowers us. 1 Samuel 16:7 "The Lord does not look at the things people look at. People look at the outward appearance, but the Lord looks at the heart." When we have a heart that trusts in God, He can do amazing things through us, just like He did with David.

In David's case, Goliath was a literal giant who seemed impossible to defeat. But Goliath represents the giants in our own lives—things that seem bigger than us and impossible to overcome. These giants can take many forms. It could be fear, addiction, insecurity, a difficult relationship, financial struggles, or even a health problem. Whatever your giant is, know that with God, you have the power to overcome it. Just like David, you can face your giants with faith, and God will help you overcome them. David's victory over Goliath teaches us several important lessons about overcoming the giants in our lives. David didn't trust in his own strength. Instead, he trusted in God's power to help him defeat Goliath. In **1 Samuel 17:45-47** David said to Goliath, *"You come against me with sword and spear, but I come against you in the name of the Lord Almighty, the God of the armies of Israel, whom you have defied."* David knew that God's power was greater than any enemy he faced. Just like David, we must place our trust in God's power, not our own abilities. God is greater than anything that stands in our way. David didn't use the armor or weapons that others thought he should use. Instead, he chose to use the simple tools he knew—his sling and five smooth stones. What David had was enough because he had faith in God. In the same way, God doesn't always call us to do things in a way that others might expect. He can use whatever we have, no matter how small, when we trust in Him. David's victory came from his confidence that God had been faithful in the past and would continue to be faithful in the future. David remembered how God helped him defeat the lion and the bear. When you face challenges, remember how God has helped you in the past. Trust that He will continue to be faithful and guide you through every battle. David didn't just talk about his faith—he acted on it. He didn't wait for Goliath to come to him. He boldly ran toward Goliath and took action. When you have faith, it moves you to take action, even when things seem impossible. David's victory was not just about defeating Goliath—it was about proving that God was faithful and that nothing is impossible with Him. The victory was already won before David even threw the stone. God had already determined the outcome, and David's faith brought that victory into reality. Romans 8:37 *"No, in all these things we are more than conquerors through him who loved us."* Through Jesus, the ultimate victory is already ours. No matter how big the battle, we can have confidence that God will bring us through and that we are more than conquerors through Him. Just like David faced Goliath with faith, you can face the giants in your life. Trust that God is bigger than your challenges. He has the power to help you overcome any obstacle. Look back on how God has helped you in the past and trust that He will do it again. Don't wait for the perfect situation. Trust that God can use what you already have to bring victory. Faith requires action. Don't just wait for things to change—take steps in faith and trust that God will guide you. Know that the battle has already been won through Jesus, and you can walk in that victory every day.

How To Remain Focused On God's Purpose Amidst Distractions

Have you ever wondered why you are here or what your life is meant for? These are questions many people ask. Thankfully, the Bible gives us clear answers. God has a purpose for every person's life, and this purpose is not random—it was planned long before we were born.

In Jeremiah 1:5, God says, *"Before I formed you in the womb I knew you, before you were born I set you apart; I appointed you as a prophet to the nations."* These words were spoken to Jeremiah, but they reflect a truth about all of us: God knew us before we were even born. He created us with love and a specific purpose in mind. God is deeply personal. He doesn't see us as just one among many; He sees us as individuals. Before you were formed in your mother's womb, God already had a plan for you. He knew your strengths, your struggles, and your potential. You are not an accident or a coincidence. You are here because God wanted you to be here. Think about that for a moment. The Creator of the universe, the One who made the stars and the earth, thought about you before you even existed. He formed you carefully, giving you unique talents, personality, and gifts. These are all part of His purpose for your life. When God told Jeremiah, *"I set you apart,"* it meant Jeremiah's life had a special calling. The same is true for you. To be set apart means that God has chosen you for something meaningful and unique. It doesn't necessarily mean you have to become a prophet like Jeremiah. God's purpose for each of us is different. It could be to teach, to serve others, to create, or to share His love with those around us. Whatever your calling is, it's important to know that it is valuable. You don't have to compare your purpose to someone else's. God's plan for you is tailored just for you. Ephesians 2:10, *"For we are God's handiwork, created in Christ Jesus to do good works, which God prepared in advance for us to do."* This verse reminds us that God has already prepared opportunities for us to fulfill our purpose. Understanding God's purpose for your life brings peace and hope. Sometimes we feel lost or unsure, but God's plans are never uncertain. Jeremiah 29:11, God promises, *"For I know the plans I have for you," declares the Lord, "plans to prosper you and not to harm you, plans to give you hope and a future."* This means God's purpose for you is always good. Even when life feels hard or confusing, He is working for your benefit. Once you begin to understand God's purpose for your life, the next step is to live it out. This requires trust and obedience. Sometimes, God's plans might lead you out of your comfort zone, but that's okay. He will give you the strength and wisdom to succeed. God never calls you to something without giving you what you need to accomplish it. He will equip you with His strength, guidance, and resources.

Colossians 3:2, *"Set your minds on things above, not on earthly things."* This means focusing on eternal things, like loving God, trusting His promises, and living in a way that honors Him. It's easy to get distracted by everyday worries or pleasures, but when we prioritize God, everything else falls into place. One way to set your heart and mind on God is to start your day with Him. Spend time in prayer, read the Bible, and reflect on His goodness. When you start your day with God, it's like setting a compass —it helps you stay on the right path. Throughout the day, keep your thoughts aligned with His promises, especially during tough moments. Remind yourself that God is with you, guiding and strengthening you. By fixing our hearts on God, we learn to value what truly matters. The things of this world are temporary, but God's love and promises are eternal. When we live with this mindset, we find peace and purpose. Distractions can come in many forms, and while some may seem harmless, they can pull us away from God if we're not careful. For example, spending too much time on social media, being overly focused on work, or worrying about the future can take our attention away from God's purpose for us. Hebrews 12:1, *"Let us throw off everything that hinders and the sin that so easily entangles. And let us run with perseverance the race marked out for us."* This verse encourages us to get rid of anything that slows us down or distracts us from our spiritual journey.

Take a moment to reflect on your life. What is keeping you from focusing on God? Is it fear, stress, or too many commitments? Once you identify these distractions, take steps to limit or remove them. For example, set boundaries on how much time you spend online, or give your worries to God through prayer. By clearing these distractions, you'll be able to focus more fully on God and His plans for you. Staying close to God is essential to keeping your focus on Him. Prayer is like having a conversation with God —it connects your heart to His. When you pray, you invite God into your struggles and victories, and He fills you with His peace. Worship is another powerful way to stay close to God. When we worship, we declare God's greatness and shift our focus from our problems to His power. Singing songs of praise, thanking God for His blessings, or simply meditating on His goodness helps to keep our hearts aligned with Him.

Make prayer and worship a daily habit. Start your mornings by thanking God, pray throughout your day, and end your evenings with gratitude. By staying connected to God in this way, you'll feel His presence and guidance, even when life gets busy. The people we surround ourselves with can either help us grow closer to God or distract us from Him. Being part of a supportive community strengthens our faith and keeps us accountable. Find people who share your faith and are committed to following God. This could be a church group, a Bible study, or close friends who pray with you and encourage you. These relationships are like a safety net —they help you stay grounded when life gets challenging and remind you of God's truths.

If you don't already have a group like this, pray and ask God to lead you to one. Having people who inspire you, pray for you, and walk alongside you in faith will make a big difference in staying focused on God's purpose. Together, you can grow stronger in your faith and make a greater impact for His kingdom.

It's easy to feel frustrated when things don't happen as quickly as we want. Maybe you've prayed for something, and it feels like God is silent. You might even be tempted to take control and try to make things happen on your own. But trusting God means believing that He knows what's best and that His timing is perfect. While we may only see a small piece of the puzzle, God knows how everything will work together for our good. When we trust God's timing, we can let go of the stress and pressure of trying to figure everything out. Instead of doubting or rushing ahead, we can pray, seek His guidance, and wait patiently. God's promises are sure, and His plan will always unfold at the perfect time. Trusting God means believing this, even when you can't yet see the outcome. Living out God's purpose requires discipline. Just like athletes train every day to win a race, we need to stay committed to our spiritual growth. 1 Corinthians 9:24-25, *"Run in such a way as to get the prize. Everyone who competes in the games goes into strict training."* This means we can't just focus on God when we feel like it; we need to stay consistent, even when it's hard. When life gets busy or distractions come, it's important to remember why we're here. God's purpose for your life is about more than just your personal success or comfort—it's about His Kingdom. He wants to use you to make a difference in the world by sharing His love, helping others, and living a life that points people to Him. Matthew 6:33, *"But seek first his kingdom and his righteousness, and all these things will be given to you as well."* This means putting God's priorities first. When we focus on His Kingdom, He takes care of everything else we need. Ask yourself, *"How can I make an impact for God's Kingdom today?"* Maybe it's by encouraging someone who is struggling, volunteering to help those in need, or simply being kind and patient in your everyday interactions. Remember, your life is part of a much bigger story, and God is using you to bring His love and light to the world. Staying focused on God's purpose means keeping your eyes on the ultimate goal: eternity with Him. This life is temporary, but what we do for God has eternal value. In 2 Timothy 4:7-8, Paul writes, *"I have fought the good fight, I have finished the race, I have kept the faith. Now there is in store for me the crown of righteousness."* Paul's words remind us that our journey of faith is like running a race. It takes effort, endurance, and focus, but the reward is worth it.

When challenges come, think about the eternal prize. The trials we face now are small compared to the joy we will experience in God's presence forever. No matter how tough things get, keep pressing forward. Stay faithful, and don't let anything distract you from the purpose God has for your life. When you keep your eyes on the prize, you'll find strength, hope, and peace to continue your journey.

The Importance Of Guarding Your Heart As You Rise To Greatness

As you pursue your dreams, grow in your faith, and rise to greatness, one of the most important things you can do is guard your heart. The heart is a key part of our life—our actions, thoughts, and attitudes all flow from it. To rise to greatness in a way that honors God and brings lasting success, you must protect your heart from things that can harm your character, your relationships, and your purpose. Proverbs 4:23, *"Above all else, guard your heart, for everything you do flows from it."* This means that your heart affects how you think, what you say, and how you act. If your heart is full of bitterness, anger, or fear, your actions will reflect that. But if your heart is full of peace, love, and faith, your actions will show that too. When you guard your heart, you are protecting the very core of who you are. As you rise to greatness, you need to make sure that your heart remains pure, focused, and aligned with God's will for your life. If you don't guard your heart, the wrong things can start to shape your behavior, and this can take you off course. There are many things that can try to harm or distract your heart, especially as you rise to greatness. These can include negative thoughts, hurtful people, or even fear and doubt. As you chase your dreams, people around you may say things that discourage you or try to stop you from moving forward. Sometimes, challenges or past failures can make you feel unworthy or fearful. But God will not to let these things control our hearts. Psalm 34:18 *"The Lord is close to the brokenhearted and saves those who are crushed in spirit."* Even when you feel discouraged or hurt, God is there to heal and protect your heart. It's important to stay close to God during difficult times, trusting that He will help you guard your heart against negativity. Rising to greatness is not just about achieving success in the world's eyes; it's about fulfilling the purpose that God has for your life. To do this, you need to keep your heart focused on His plan for you. This means spending time with Him, praying, reading the Bible, and listening to His guidance. When your heart is in tune with God's will, He can lead you to greatness in a way that honors Him.

As you grow and succeed, it can be easy to become proud or boastful. You might start to think that you've done everything on your own or that you don't need God as much. But pride can lead to downfall. Proverbs 16:18, *"Pride goes before destruction, a haughty spirit before a fall."* When you allow pride to enter your heart, it can cause you to make decisions that are not in line with God's will. To guard your heart against pride, always remember that it is God who gives you the strength and wisdom to succeed. Keep a humble heart and give God the glory for every victory. Humility is key to continuing on the path to greatness without losing sight of God's purpose for your life. As you rise to greatness, you may be tempted to compare your life to others. You might look at someone else's success and feel discouraged because your journey seems different or slower. But comparison can steal your joy and cause you to lose focus on your own unique path. Galatians 6:4-5, *"Each one should test their own actions. Then they can take pride in themselves alone, without comparing themselves to someone else, for each one should carry their own load."* When you focus on your own journey and what God has called you to do, you will avoid the trap of comparison. Your greatness is unique to you, and it's not about measuring up to others but following God's plan for your life. One of the biggest things that can affect your heart as you rise to greatness is unforgiveness. Holding on to anger or bitterness towards others can weigh you down and prevent you from moving forward. Forgiveness is a key part of guarding your heart. As you move forward in life, there will always be people who hurt you. But letting go of grudges and choosing to forgive others will keep your heart free and open to God's blessings. God's forgiveness of us is a powerful reminder that we should forgive others as well. A pure heart is a heart that is free from wrong desires, harmful thoughts, and anything that would separate us from God. To rise to greatness in a way that honors God, you must keep your heart pure. Matthew 5:8 *"Blessed are the pure in heart, for they will see God."* When you live with a pure heart, you allow God to work through you in powerful ways. To maintain purity in your heart, avoid filling your mind with negative influences. Protect yourself from things like harmful media, bad company, or sinful habits that can corrupt your heart. Instead, focus on things that are good, pure, and pleasing to God. One of the best ways to guard your heart as you rise to greatness is through prayer and worship. These practices keep you connected to God, and they help you stay focused on His will. Through prayer and worship, you invite God's peace into your heart. His peace will protect you from anxiety, fear, and distractions that can lead you away from His purpose for your life.

CHAPTER 10

UNDERSTANDING THE SPIRITUAL WARFARE AROUND YOU

Spiritual warfare is the unseen battle between good and evil, where God fights for us against forces that try to pull us away from Him. It's not just a physical struggle but a spiritual one, happening in our hearts, minds, and lives. When we read Job 41, we see a description of Leviathan, a mighty and untamable creature. Leviathan can represent spiritual strongholds—things that are hard to break free from in our lives. Spiritual warfare is the fight between God's kingdom and the enemy's forces. Ephesians 6:12, "For our struggle is not against flesh and blood, but against the rulers, against the authorities, against the powers of this dark world and against the spiritual forces of evil in the heavenly realms." This means that while we may face challenges like fear, temptation, or conflict, the root of these struggles is often spiritual. The enemy uses lies, doubts, and distractions to keep us from living for God. In Job 41, Leviathan is described as a massive sea creature, full of power and hard to control. God uses this creature to show Job how small humans are compared to His might. Leviathan can also represent spiritual strongholds—things that feel impossible to defeat on our own. A stronghold might be fear, addiction, anger, or even a negative mindset. Just like Leviathan is too powerful for humans to handle alone, these strongholds can seem impossible to break free from without God.

Here are some descriptions of Leviathan and what they teach us about spiritual strongholds. In Job 41:10 it says, *"No one is fierce enough to rouse it. Who then is able to stand against me?"* This reminds us that spiritual battles are not something we can win by ourselves. We need God's help. In Job 41:34 Leviathan is called the *"king over all that are proud."* Pride can be a major stronghold in our lives, making us rely on ourselves instead of God. The description of Leviathan's strength shows that strongholds can cause destruction in our lives—damaging relationships, stealing our peace, and keeping us far from God.

A spiritual stronghold is a place in your life where the enemy has built control. These strongholds are like fortresses of lies or bad habits that are hard to tear down. Constant worry and anxiety can take over your thoughts, making it hard to trust God. Repeated sins, like dishonesty or jealousy, can trap us in guilt and shame. Holding onto grudges can become a barrier between us and God's peace. Questioning God's love or plan for our lives can make us feel lost and stuck. 2 Corinthians 10:4-5, *"The weapons we fight with are not the weapons of the world. On the contrary, they have divine power to demolish strongholds. We demolish arguments and every pretension that sets itself up against the knowledge of God."* This shows that God gives us the power to tear down these strongholds. While Leviathan reminds us of the power of strongholds, God's Word shows us how to fight these battles and find freedom. Paul talks about the armor of God, which includes truth, righteousness, the gospel of peace, faith, salvation, and the Word of God. . Ephesians 6:13-17. These are spiritual tools that protect us and help us fight against the enemy. Strongholds often begin with lies from the enemy, like "You're not good enough" or "God doesn't love you." We fight these lies by speaking God's truth. For example, when we feel unloved, we can declare Romans 8:38-39, which says nothing can separate us from God's love. In Job 41, God shows Job that only He has the power to control Leviathan. Similarly, we must surrender our strongholds to God because only He can break them. One of the most important lessons from Job 41 is that God is greater than anything we face. Leviathan may be untamable for humans, but it is no match for God. Similarly, our strongholds may seem overwhelming, but God has the power to set us free. Isaiah 27:1 it says, *"In that day, the Lord will punish with his sword —his fierce, great and powerful sword—Leviathan the gliding serpent, Leviathan the coiling serpent; he will slay the monster of the sea."* This verse reminds us that God will defeat every stronghold and enemy that stands against us. Once God helps us break free from strongholds, we must continue to live in freedom. This means staying close to God through prayer, reading His Word, and trusting Him daily. It also means resisting the temptation to fall back into old patterns. True freedom comes through Jesus, and it lasts when we stay connected to Him.

Recognizing And Dealing With The Spiritual Forces That Oppose Your Destiny

Spiritual forces are powers and influences in the spiritual realm that affect our thoughts, emotions, and actions. These forces are not seen with our eyes, but they are real and can affect our lives. The Bible talks about two main types of spiritual forces: good forces (angels, God's Holy Spirit) and evil forces (demons, Satan). Dealing with these forces is to recognize them. Spiritual forces that oppose your destiny usually show up in different ways. One of the most common tactics of the enemy is to make you doubt God's plan for your life. He will try to tell you that you are not good enough, that your dreams are too big, or that you can never succeed. If you start to feel hopeless or doubtful about your future, this may be a spiritual attack. Fear is another spiritual force that tries to stop you from moving forward. Fear can make you avoid taking steps toward your destiny, keep you stuck in comfort, or cause you to be anxious about the unknown. Fear is not from God. Temptation is when the enemy tries to pull you away from God's path by tempting you to sin or make bad choices. These temptations can be distractions that take you off course or things that seem appealing in the moment but lead to destruction. Temptation is dangerous, and it's important to recognize it and resist it. Unforgiveness can block your progress in fulfilling your destiny. When you hold on to hurt and bitterness, it's like a chain that keeps you stuck in the past. The enemy uses unforgiveness to keep you in bondage, preventing you from moving forward in God's plan. Forgiving others is a key to unlocking freedom and moving forward in God's destiny for your life.

Now that we recognize the spiritual forces that oppose our destiny, it's important to know how to deal with them. Here are some steps to help you overcome the spiritual forces that try to stop you: Prayer is a powerful weapon against the spiritual forces that oppose you. When you pray, you invite God's power into your situation, and He helps you overcome the enemy. Speaking God's Word out loud is also powerful. The Bible says that the Word of God is like a sword that defeats the enemy. Ephesians 6:17 *"Take the helmet of salvation and the sword of the Spirit, which is the word of God."* Whenever you feel attacked by spiritual forces, pray and declare God's promises over your life. The Bible says that we should resist the devil and he will flee from us. You have the authority in Christ to stand firm and say no to the devil. Resist his lies, temptations, and discouragements, and trust that God will give you victory. God has given us armor to protect us from the enemy's attacks. In Ephesians 6:10-18 Paul talks about the armor of God, which includes truth, righteousness, peace, faith, salvation, and the Word of God. By putting on this armor, you are prepared to face spiritual battles. Every day, take time to pray and put on the armor of God so that you are ready to resist the enemy. Knowing who you are in Christ is key to overcoming spiritual forces. The enemy will try to make you forget your identity as a child of God, but when you remember that you are loved, forgiven, and empowered by God, you can stand strong. 1 Peter 2:9 *"But you are a chosen people, a royal priesthood, a holy nation, God's special possession, that you may declare the praises of him who called you out of darkness into his wonderful light."* Remember who you are in Christ, and let that truth guide your actions. As mentioned earlier, unforgiveness is a spiritual force that can hold you back. It's important to forgive others as God has forgiven you. Holding onto anger and bitterness can keep you from moving forward in God's plan. To overcome spiritual forces and fulfill your destiny, you must keep your eyes on Jesus. He is the author and perfecter of our faith (Hebrews 12:2). When we focus on Him, we receive the strength and grace we need to overcome every challenge.

How To Wage Spiritual Warfare With God's Weapons

Spiritual warfare is the battle between good and evil that takes place in the unseen spiritual realm. Our enemy is not other people, but evil spiritual forces that try to influence us to turn away from God. The good news is that God has given us weapons to fight this battle and win. These weapons are not physical weapons, like swords or guns, but spiritual weapons that are powerful and effective in defeating the enemy. One of the most important weapons in spiritual warfare is the Word of God. The Bible is called the "sword of the Spirit" because it is powerful and sharp. In Ephesians 6:17 *"Take the helmet of salvation and the sword of the Spirit, which is the word of God."*

God's Word is powerful and can defeat the lies of the enemy. When Jesus was tempted by Satan in the wilderness, He used God's Word to resist the devil. God's Word is a strong weapon that we can use to fight against temptation and deception. When you face difficult situations or when the enemy tries to make you doubt, speak God's Word over those situations. For example, when you feel afraid, you can say, *"God has not given me a spirit of fear, but of power, love, and a sound mind"* (2 Timothy 1:7). In Ephesians 6:18 Paul encourages believers to *"pray in the Spirit on all occasions with all kinds of prayers and requests."* Prayer connects us with God and allows us to ask for His help in the battle. Through prayer, we invite God's power into our lives and situations. When we pray, God listens, and He answers according to His will. Prayer is a way to fight against the enemy by seeking God's strength, wisdom, and intervention. When you are under attack, pray with authority and confidence. Ask God to protect you, to give you strength, and to help you stand firm against the enemy.

Faith is a strong weapon in spiritual warfare. In Ephesians 6:16 *"Take up the shield of faith, with which you can extinguish all the flaming arrows of the evil one."* The enemy will try to attack you with lies, doubts, and fears, but your faith in God will protect you. Just like a shield protects a soldier from arrows, faith protects you from the attacks of the enemy.

When the enemy tries to make you doubt God's promises or God's goodness, you can raise your shield of faith and trust that God will do what He has promised. Hebrews 11:1 *"Now faith is confidence in what we hope for and assurance about what we do not see."* Even when you don't see the answer to your prayers right away, keep trusting God. Faith in God's promises is a powerful weapon in spiritual warfare. The helmet of salvation protects your mind. Ephesians 6:17 Paul to *"take the helmet of salvation"* as part of our spiritual armor. Salvation is the knowledge that you are saved by Jesus and that nothing can separate you from God's love. This truth protects your mind from the enemy's lies and confusion. When the enemy tries to attack your thoughts with doubt or discouragement, remember that you are saved and loved by God. You are a child of God, and nothing can take that away. Keep your mind focused on this truth, and let it guard your thoughts. The breastplate of righteousness protects your heart. Ephesians 6:14 *"Stand firm then, with the belt of truth buckled around your waist, with the breastplate of righteousness in place."* Righteousness means being in right standing with God through Jesus Christ. When you live a life that honors God, you protect your heart from the attacks of the enemy. If you fall into sin, don't let it bring guilt and shame. Instead, confess your sin and ask God for forgiveness. Praise and worship are also powerful weapons in spiritual warfare. When you worship God, you invite His presence into your life, and the enemy has no power where God's presence is. Psalm 22:3 *"Yet you are enthroned as the Holy One; you are the one Israel praises."* When we praise God, we acknowledge His power and majesty, and the enemy has to flee. The name of Jesus is one of the most powerful weapons in spiritual warfare. Philippians 2:10-11 *"That at the name of Jesus every knee should bow, in heaven and on earth and under the earth, and every tongue acknowledge that Jesus Christ is Lord."* The name of Jesus has power over every evil force.

When you face spiritual battles, speak the name of Jesus. Command the enemy to leave, and declare that the victory is yours in Jesus' name.

CHAPTER 11

CUTTING OFF THE CANCEROUS FORCES IN YOUR LIFE

In life, there are many things that can weigh us down or hold us back, preventing us from living the life God has planned for us. These things can be harmful, like cancer in the body, spreading and causing destruction. But just as doctors treat cancer to heal the body, God offers spiritual deliverance to remove harmful forces from our lives. These "cancerous forces" can be negative habits, bad relationships, unforgiveness, sin, or even destructive thoughts that pull us away from God's purpose. Cutting off these forces is essential for experiencing spiritual breakthrough and living in God's freedom. The term "cancerous forces" refers to anything that slowly eats away at your spiritual health, steals your peace, and keeps you from experiencing God's best. These forces could be: Sin, Unforgiveness, Negative relationships, Addictions or bad habits, Fear and doubt, Generational curses. Just like cancer in the body, these spiritual forces can start small, but if they are not dealt with, they can grow and cause serious damage. They block you from experiencing the fullness of God's love, peace, and victory. God doesn't want us to live under the control of these harmful forces. He desires for us to experience spiritual freedom and victory. John 10:10, "The thief comes only to steal and kill and destroy; I have come that they may have life, and have it to the full." Jesus came to give us life, and that life is free from the bondage of sin, fear, and anything that holds us back. Ephesians 4:22-24 "put off your old self, which is being corrupted by its deceitful desires; to be made new in the attitude of your minds; and to put on the new self, created to be like God in true righteousness and holiness." This is a call to remove the harmful things in our lives and put on what God has for us, which leads to spiritual growth and breakthrough.

The process of cutting off cancerous forces involves both spiritual action and trust in God's power. To cut off any harmful force is to recognize it. You need to be honest with yourself and identify areas where you are struggling or being attacked. In Psalm 139:23-24 David prayed, *"Search me, God, and know my heart; test me and know my anxious thoughts. See if there is any offensive way in me, and lead me in the way everlasting."* Ask God to show you areas where you need healing or freedom. Repentance is when you turn away from sin and return to God. It means asking God for forgiveness and choosing to live differently. When you repent, God cleanses you and breaks the power of sin over your life. Unforgiveness is a major spiritual cancer. It keeps you stuck in the past and prevents God's healing in your life. Matthew 6:14-15, *"For if you forgive other people when they sin against you, your heavenly Father will also forgive you. But if you do not forgive others their sins, your Father will not forgive your sins."* Forgiving others sets you free from the bitterness and pain that can hold you captive. Renouncing means to officially reject or give up something. In the spiritual sense, it's important to renounce the negative forces and behaviors that have been controlling you. This includes rejecting the lies of the enemy, such as fear, shame, or rejection. In James 4:7 *"Submit yourselves, then, to God. Resist the devil, and he will flee from you."* When you resist the enemy and renounce the negative forces, they lose their power over your life. Prayer is a powerful tool in cutting off harmful forces. Mark 9:29, *"This kind can come out only by prayer."* There are times when specific deliverance is needed to break free from spiritual strongholds. Pray and ask God to set you free from any harmful forces in your life. Trust in His power to deliver you. God created us to live in community. Surrounding yourself with supportive and godly people can help you stay strong and focused on God's truth. In Being part of a strong Christian community gives you the encouragement and accountability needed to stay on track. God's Word is your greatest weapon against the enemy. It has the power to break chains and bring deliverance. Hebrews 4:12 says, *"For the word of God is alive and active. Sharper than any double-edged sword, it penetrates even to dividing soul and spirit, joints and marrow; it judges the thoughts and attitudes of the heart."* Spend time in God's Word daily, and let it transform your mind and heart. Once you have cut off the cancerous forces in your life, it's important to walk in the freedom God has given you. Galatians 5:1 says, *"It is for freedom that Christ has set us free. Stand firm, then, and do not let yourselves be burdened again by a yoke of slavery."* Walk in the victory and freedom that Jesus won for you. God promises that He will deliver us from all forms of bondage and oppression.

How God Empowers You To Sever Unhealthy Influences

God wants the best for you, and part of His plan for your life is to help you live free from unhealthy influences that can hold you back. These influences can be spiritual, emotional, or physical, and they can weigh you down, causing pain and preventing you from living fully in God's purpose. But the good news is that God empowers you to sever, or cut off, these unhealthy influences, so you can walk in freedom and experience His peace and joy. Unhealthy influences are anything in your life that affects you in a way that pulls you away from God, harms your growth, or hurts your well-being. These influences can come in different forms, and they may not always be obvious at first. But over time, they can impact how you think, feel, and live.

- **Spiritual Influences:** These are things that negatively affect your relationship with God and your spiritual walk. Thinking things that don't align with God's Word, like believing you're not good enough for God's love. Situations or desires that encourage you to disobey God. Spending too much time with people who lead you away from God instead of toward Him. For example, if you surround yourself with people who don't value godly principles, their influence can make it harder for you to stay strong in your faith. The Bible warns us in 1 Corinthians 15:33 *"Do not be misled: 'Bad company corrupts good character.'"*
- **Emotional Influences:** Emotional influences affect your heart and mind. Emotions like anger, bitterness, or fear that weigh you down. Painful experiences that make it hard to trust or feel peace. People who make you feel unworthy, unloved, or unsafe. Emotional wounds can keep you stuck, making it hard to move forward or enjoy the blessings God has for you. For instance, holding on to bitterness can block you from experiencing joy and forgiveness. Ephesians 4:31-32 *"Get rid of all bitterness, rage, and anger... Be kind and compassionate to one another, forgiving each other, just as in Christ God forgave you."*
- **Physical Influences:** These include habits, environments, or addictions that harm your body, which is a gift from God. Things like overeating, lack of exercise, or not taking care of your body. Spending time in places where you're tempted to sin or feel unsafe. Struggles like substance abuse or any habit that controls your life. 1 Corinthians 6:19-20 *"Do you not know that your bodies are temples of the Holy Spirit, who is in you...? You are not your own; you were bought at a price. Therefore honor God with your bodies."*

Unhealthy influences can feel overwhelming, but God gives us the power to overcome them. Ask God to show you anything in your life that's not good for you. Sometimes, these influences can be hidden, but prayer and reflection can bring them to light. Psalm 139:23-24 *"Search me, God, and know my heart; test me and know my anxious thoughts. See if there is any offensive way in me, and lead me in the way everlasting."* Once you recognize an unhealthy influence, take steps to remove it. It might mean ending a toxic relationship, changing a habit, or avoiding certain environments. Fill your life with positive influences that strengthen your relationship with God. Surround yourself with supportive people, focus on God's Word, and practice healthy habits. You don't have to do this alone. God gives you the strength to overcome. When you let go of unhealthy influences, you open the door for God to work in your life. You'll experience more peace, joy, and purpose. God wants you to live a full and abundant life, free from the things that hold you back. John 10:10 *"The thief comes only to steal and kill and destroy; I have come that they may have life, and have it to the full."* By breaking free from unhealthy influences, you can fully embrace the life God has planned for you—one filled with love, growth, and victory.

Trust God to guide you, strengthen you, and help you walk in freedom. Let His truth lead you away from the things that harm you and closer to the life He created you to live. One of the key ways God empowers you is through His strength. On your own, you may feel weak or unable to make changes. But with God's help, you can overcome anything that tries to hold you back.

Changing your thoughts pattern is the first step to cutting off unhealthy influences Sometimes, unhealthy influences start in your mind—wrong beliefs, lies, and negative thoughts that hold you back. God empowers you to renew your mind by replacing those lies with His truth. Romans 12:2 *"Do not conform to the pattern of this world, but be transformed by the renewing of your mind."* When your mind is renewed by God's Word, you start seeing things from His perspective. You begin to understand what is good for you, what is harmful, and what God's will is for your life. This change in thinking helps you recognize the unhealthy influences and gives you the wisdom to remove them from your life. God's Word is powerful. It helps you discern between what is good and what is harmful. It is like a sword that can cut through the lies and negative influences in your life. By reading and speaking God's Word, you strengthen yourself and resist the things that try to pull you away from His will. When you face temptations, emotional struggles, or unhealthy habits, God's Word can give you the power to resist. It reminds you of your true identity in Christ and helps you stay focused on what is good and true. The Holy Spirit is another way God empowers you to sever unhealthy influences. The Holy Spirit lives inside you and helps you make wise choices, gives you strength to resist temptation, and comforts you when you are hurting. He guides you in making decisions that will protect you from harmful influences. John 14:26 *"But the Advocate, the Holy Spirit, whom the Father will send in my name, will teach you all things and will remind you of everything I have said to you."* The Holy Spirit gives you the wisdom and strength you need to break free from things that aren't good for you. When you listen to His voice, He leads you away from unhealthy influences and towards a life that honors God.

Sometimes, unhealthy influences come from the people around us. Whether it's friends, family members, or acquaintances, toxic relationships can affect your spiritual, emotional, and even physical well-being. These relationships may cause you to doubt God, feel depressed, or even encourage you to sin.

God empowers you to recognize these toxic relationships and, when necessary, sever them for your health and spiritual growth. 1 Corinthians 15:33 *"Do not be misled: 'Bad company corrupts good character.'"* God's Word teaches that the people you associate with can influence your life, so you must choose your relationships wisely. While God calls you to love everyone, He doesn't call you to let anyone lead you away from Him or cause harm to you emotionally or spiritually. Trust God to give you the courage to set boundaries or distance yourself from unhealthy relationships, while continuing to love those around you. Many people struggle with physical addictions or bad habits that harm their bodies and their relationship with God. These could be things like unhealthy eating, substance abuse, or other forms of addiction that control your life. These addictions are difficult to break, but God empowers you to overcome them. 1 Corinthians 10:13 *"No temptation has overtaken you except what is common to mankind. And God is faithful; he will not let you be tempted beyond what you can bear. But when you are tempted, he will also provide a way out so that you can endure it."* God promises that He will never leave you alone in your struggle. He provides a way for you to break free from anything that controls you. Through prayer, accountability, and support from others, you can find freedom from these unhealthy influences. God is faithful to help you overcome addictions and habits that are harmful to your body, mind, and spirit. Emotional wounds, like hurt from the past, anger, unforgiveness, or feelings of worthlessness, can also be an unhealthy influence in your life. These wounds can prevent you from experiencing the fullness of God's love and joy. But God empowers you to heal and be free from these emotional scars. Psalm 34:18 *"The Lord is close to the brokenhearted and saves those who are crushed in spirit."* God sees your pain and wants to heal you. When you bring your emotional wounds to Him, He can heal your heart and help you sever the unhealthy patterns of thinking that come from hurt. Forgiveness is also a key part of emotional healing. In Ephesians 4:31-32 *"Get rid of all bitterness, rage and anger, brawling and slander, along with every form of malice. Be kind and compassionate to one another, forgiving each other, just as in Christ God forgave you."* When you forgive those who have hurt you, God releases you from the grip of bitterness and anger, helping you heal emotionally and spiritually.

Walking In Freedom And Victory In Every Area Of Your Life

As believers in Jesus Christ, we are called to live in freedom and victory. God doesn't want us to be trapped by fear, sin, or any other obstacles. He wants us to experience His power and live fully in His promises. But how do we walk in freedom and victory in every area of our lives? Freedom in Christ is more than just being free from physical chains or struggles. It's about being free in our hearts and minds. When we accept Jesus into our lives, He sets us free from sin, fear, guilt, shame, and anything that holds us back. John 8:36 , *"So if the Son sets you free, you will be free indeed."* This means that when we follow Jesus, He gives us real freedom —freedom from the things that try to control us. This freedom isn't just for a moment, but for our whole lives. One of the areas where we need freedom is from sin. Sin can make us feel stuck, but when we accept Jesus, He gives us the power to break free from it. Jesus died on the cross to set us free from the power of sin. Through His sacrifice, we can choose to live according to God's ways. Romans 6:14 *"For sin shall no longer be your master, because you are not under the law, but under grace."* This means that sin no longer has control over us. We have the choice to say no to sin and live in victory. Another area where many people struggle is fear and anxiety. Life can be difficult, and we may worry about the future, our health, or our finances. But God wants us to be free from fear. He promises to be with us through every situation, and His presence gives us peace. God has given us His power and love to face any challenge with confidence. Our minds are powerful, and sometimes we can feel trapped by negative thoughts. These can be thoughts of failure, unworthiness, or fear about the future. But God's Word helps us take control of our thoughts and think in a positive, God-honoring way. Philippians 4:8 Paul encourages us, *"Finally, brothers and sisters, whatever is true, whatever is noble, whatever is right, whatever is pure, whatever is lovely, whatever is admirable—if anything is excellent or praiseworthy—think about such things."* When we focus on God's truth, we can overcome negative thinking and experience peace and victory.

Freedom and victory also apply to our relationships. God wants us to have healthy, loving relationships with others, whether it's with family, friends, or colleagues. Sometimes, we can experience conflict, hurt, or brokenness in relationships, but God can heal and restore them. God wants us to forgive, be kind, and show love to others, just as He has forgiven and loved us. When we walk in forgiveness and love, our relationships can be healed and restored. Life is not always easy, and we will face challenges, trials, and difficulties. However, God promises that He will be with us through it all. He gives us the strength to overcome every challenge and experience victory. Romans 8:37 *"No, in all these things we are more than conquerors through him who loved us."* Even when we face difficult situations, we can be confident that with God's help, we will overcome. We are not just survivors; we are more than conquerors in Christ. Living in freedom and victory also means living in God's purpose for our lives. God has a plan for each of us, and when we follow His leading, we experience true fulfillment. Walking in God's purpose helps us find joy and peace in our daily lives. One of the keys to walking in freedom and victory is learning to live by the Holy Spirit. The Holy Spirit guides us, strengthens us, and empowers us to live the life God has called us to live. When we walk in the Spirit, we can experience victory in every area of our lives. Galatians 5:16, *"So I say, walk by the Spirit, and you will not gratify the desires of the flesh."* When we follow the Holy Spirit's guidance, we can avoid the traps of sin and live in the freedom that God has for us.

PART 4

EMBRACING YOUR SUPERNATURAL CALLING

"God has called you to serve Him in a way that no one else can. Do not neglect that calling, for it is uniquely yours, and it comes with the power of the Holy Spirit to accomplish the tasks He has set before you." Charles Spurgeon

"Therefore, I, a prisoner for serving the Lord, beg you to lead a life worthy of your calling, for you have been called by God. Always be humble and gentle. Be patient with each other, making allowance for each other's faults because of your love." Ephesians 4:1-2 (NLT)

CHAPTER 12

RISING TO YOUR FULL POTENTIAL IN GOD

You are not here by accident. God created you for a specific purpose. He has placed you in this world to make a difference. Understanding His purpose starts with knowing that you are loved, chosen, and called by Him. To rise to your full potential, ask God to show you His purpose for your life. Spend time in prayer and His Word, listening to His guidance. God's promises in the Bible are like seeds planted in your heart. When you believe in them, they begin to grow and bear fruit in your life. His promises include peace, strength, wisdom, and success. God promises to give you strength to overcome challenges. When you trust in God's promises, you can face any challenge with confidence, knowing that He is with you every step of the way. God has given you gifts and talents to use for His glory. These are not just for yourself but to bless others and make a positive impact in the world. 1 Peter 4:10 "Each of you should use whatever gift you have received to serve others, as faithful stewards of God's grace in its various forms." To rise to your potential, discover your gifts, and work on developing them. Sometimes, it can feel hard to move forward because of challenges or fears. But remember, God has already given you victory through Jesus Christ. Obstacles are not meant to stop you; they are opportunities for growth and trust in God. With God's help, you can overcome any difficulty and rise to your full potential. When fear or doubt tries to hold you back, remind yourself of God's promises. Pray, believe, and keep moving forward.

Living out your potential requires faith and obedience to God. Faith means trusting that God knows what is best for you, even when you don't understand the full picture. Obedience means following His instructions, even when it feels hard. Proverbs 3:5-6 *"Trust in the Lord with all your heart and lean not on your own understanding; in all your ways submit to him, and he will make your paths straight."* When you trust and obey God, He leads you to places you never imagined. Rising to your full potential doesn't happen overnight. It's a journey, and God works on His perfect timeline. Sometimes, you may feel impatient, but trust that God knows the right time for everything. God is shaping you, preparing you, and growing you for the right season. Be patient and stay faithful. When you live in your full potential, you become a light to the world. Your life inspires others, and you play a part in bringing God's kingdom to earth. Jesus said in Matthew 5:16 *"Let your light shine before others, that they may see your good deeds and glorify your Father in heaven."* Your actions, words, and choices can draw people closer to God and show them His love and power. God's promises for your future are full of hope and joy. He has planned blessings, opportunities, and victories for you. Trusting Him with your future means giving Him control and believing He will lead you to the best path. Psalm 32:8 God promises, *"I will instruct you and teach you in the way you should go; I will counsel you with my loving eye on you."* He is a faithful guide who will never leave you.

How To Walk In The Fullness Of God's Destiny For Your Life

God has an amazing plan for your life. He created you with a purpose, and His desire is for you to live a life filled with meaning, joy, and impact. Walking in the fullness of God's destiny means understanding His plans, following His guidance, and trusting Him every step of the way. The first step to walking in God's destiny is to believe that He has a special plan for your life. You are not here by accident. God made you with care and purpose, and His plan for you is good. To fully experience God's plan, you need to give Him control of your life. This means trusting Him with your decisions, desires, and future. When you surrender to God, you allow Him to guide you in the right direction. Knowing God's plan for your life requires spending time with Him. You can do this by praying, reading the Bible, and worshiping. When you draw closer to God, He reveals His purpose to you. God has given you unique talents, skills, and passions to fulfill your purpose. These gifts are tools to help you make a difference in the world and walk in His destiny for your life.

Obedience is key to walking in God's plan. Sometimes, God may ask you to step out of your comfort zone or do things that don't make sense right away. Trust Him and obey His guidance, knowing that He sees the bigger picture. Isaiah 1:19 *"If you are willing and obedient, you will eat the good things of the land."* Obedience brings blessings and keeps you on track with God's purpose for your life. God's plan unfolds in His perfect timing, not ours. It's easy to become impatient or feel discouraged when things don't happen as quickly as we'd like. However, God knows the right time for everything in your life. Trust that God's timing is perfect and wait on Him with faith and patience. Walking in God's destiny doesn't mean life will always be easy. You may face challenges, setbacks, or doubts. But remember, God is with you, and He will help you overcome any obstacle. Romans 8:28 *"And we know that in all things God works for the good of those who love him, who have been called according to his purpose."* Even when life gets tough, trust that God is using every situation to shape you and move you closer to His plan. The people around you can have a big impact on your journey. Surround yourself with friends, mentors, and a church community that will encourage you, pray for you, and guide you toward God's purpose. Hebrews 10:24-25 *"And let us consider how we may spur one another on toward love and good deeds, not giving up meeting together, as some are in the habit of doing, but encouraging one another."* A strong support system helps you stay focused and motivated. Sometimes, walking in God's plan requires taking bold steps of faith. You may not have all the answers, but trust that God will lead you as you move forward. Faith is believing in what you can't yet see but trusting that God is already at work. 2 Corinthians 5:7 *"For we live by faith, not by sight."* Don't let fear hold you back. Take the steps God is calling you to, knowing that He will provide what you need. As you follow God's plan, take time to celebrate the progress you make. Each step of obedience, each answered prayer, and each moment of growth is a victory. Thank God for His faithfulness and keep moving forward. 1 Thessalonians 5:18 *"Give thanks in all circumstances; for this is God's will for you in Christ Jesus."* Gratitude helps you stay positive and focused on God's goodness. God's destiny for your life is worth pursuing, even when the journey gets tough. Keep pressing forward, trusting that He will give you the strength to finish what He started.

CHAPTER 13

LIVING AS A SPIRITUAL POWERHOUSE

A spiritual powerhouse is someone who carries the presence of God wherever they go. This person walks in faith, relies on the power of the Holy Spirit, and makes a difference in the world for Jesus Christ. They are not perfect, but they are fully surrendered to God's plan for their lives. Zechariah 4:6 "Not by might nor by power, but by my Spirit." This verse reminds us that true spiritual power does not come from our own strength or abilities. It comes from God working in and through us by the Holy Spirit. Before Jesus returned to heaven, He made a promise to His disciples. He told them they would receive power when the Holy Spirit came upon them. This promise was fulfilled on the day of Pentecost, as recorded in Acts 2. When the Holy Spirit came upon the disciples, they were transformed. They were no longer afraid or unsure of what to do. Instead, they became bold and fearless, ready to share the message of Jesus with the world. The Holy Spirit gave them supernatural gifts and abilities. Wisdom to speak the truth with clarity. Courage to face persecution and danger. The power to perform miracles, healing the sick and delivering people from evil spirits. The same Holy Spirit who empowered the disciples is available to all believers today. He equips us to live victorious lives and share God's love with the world. When the Holy Spirit works in your life, He doesn't just empower you for ministry; He also transforms you from the inside out. He helps you develop the fruit of the Spirit, which are qualities that reflect God's character. Love, joy, peace, patience, kindness, goodness, faithfulness, gentleness, and self-control (Galatians 5:22-23).

These qualities make your life a testimony of God's power and goodness. People around you will notice the difference and be drawn to Christ. In the book of Acts, we see examples of how the apostles' lives were transformed, and how they, in turn, helped others experience God's power: Peter and John healed a lame man at the temple gate (*Acts 3:1-10*). This miracle showed that God's power is real and pointed people to Jesus. Philip shared the gospel in Samaria, where many people believed in Jesus and experienced healing and freedom (*Acts 8:4-8*). Paul and Silas prayed and worshipped while in prison, and their faith led to the salvation of the jailer and his entire family (*Acts 16:25-34*). When you live as a spiritual powerhouse, you allow God to use you to bring healing, hope, and salvation to others. You become a vessel through which His power flows.

To live as a spiritual powerhouse, here are some steps you can take. Spend time with God daily through prayer, Bible study, and worship. The more you connect with Him, the more His Spirit fills and empowers you. John 15:5 *"I am the vine; you are the branches. If you remain in me and I in you, you will bear much fruit; apart from me you can do nothing."* Trust God's promises and follow His instructions, even when it's difficult or doesn't make sense. Faith activates God's power in your life. Don't try to do everything in your own strength. Ask the Holy Spirit to guide, strengthen, and empower you. Remember Zechariah 4:6 *"Not by might nor by power, but by my Spirit."* God has given each believer unique gifts to serve others and glorify Him. Ask God to reveal your gifts and use them to build His kingdom. Be a witness for Christ wherever you go. Trust the Holy Spirit to give you the words and courage to share your faith with others. When you live as a spiritual powerhouse, your life becomes a light in a dark world. You reflect

God's love, bring hope to the hopeless, and help others experience the transforming power of Jesus. Just as the apostles turned the world upside down with their faith and boldness, you too can make an impact. God has placed you in your family, community, and workplace for a reason. Through the power of the Holy Spirit, you can influence those around you and advance God's kingdom on earth.

Ephesians 3:20 *"Now to him who is able to do immeasurably more than all we ask or imagine, according to his power that is at work within us."* As a spiritual powerhouse, you are part of God's plan to bring His love, truth, and salvation to the world. Trust Him, rely on His Spirit, and watch Him do amazing things through your life. To walk boldly in faith means to live with confidence and courage, trusting that God is with you no matter what. The apostles in the book of Acts are great examples of this. They spoke about Jesus openly, even when it was dangerous. They didn't let fear stop them because they knew they had God's Spirit to guide and empower them. Acts 4:13, *"When they saw the courage of Peter and John and realized that they were unschooled, ordinary men, they were astonished and took note that these men had been with Jesus."* Peter and John were not special by the world's standards—they weren't highly educated or powerful—but their boldness came from spending time with Jesus and being filled with the Holy Spirit. This shows us that we don't need to rely on our own abilities. Instead, we can depend on God to help us live boldly.

The Holy Spirit gives you power, wisdom, and courage. When you feel unqualified or scared, remember that the same Spirit who empowered the apostles lives in you. 2 Timothy 1:7 *"For the Spirit God gave us does not make us timid, but gives us power, love, and self-discipline."* Living boldly means trusting God enough to take risks for Him. Whether it's sharing your faith, standing up for what's right, or helping someone in need, God can use your obedience to make a difference. When you face fear or doubt, remind yourself of God's promises. He has said, *"I will never leave you nor forsake you"* (Hebrews 13:5) and *"If God is for us, who can be against us?"* (Romans 8:31). The early believers gathered in unity to seek God's guidance and strength (Acts 1:14). Peter prayed for Dorcas, and she was raised to life: This shows the power of praying with faith (Acts 9:40). Paul and Silas worshipped in prison, and their chains fell off: Worship invites God's power into impossible situations (Acts 16:25-26). Through prayer, you share your heart with God, and through worship, you give Him praise and honor. Both help you stay strong, no matter what challenges come your way. Even a few minutes of prayer and worship can transform your day. Whether it's a big decision or a small worry, talk to God about it. Thank God for who He is and what He has done. Worship helps shift your focus from your problems to God's greatness. Living boldly in faith isn't something you do alone. God designed us to grow and thrive in community. The early church in Acts 2:42-47 is a beautiful example of this: They prayed together. They shared meals and supported each other. They encouraged one another to stay focused on God's mission. Being part of a community helps you stay strong, especially when life gets hard. Your faith grows when you're surrounded by people who pray with you, share God's Word, and hold you accountable. The apostles didn't keep their faith to themselves. They went beyond their hometowns to share the gospel with others, transforming lives through the power of the Holy Spirit. They healed the sick, encouraged the hopeless, and brought people to Christ.

You, too, can make an impact. Whether it's reaching your family, workplace, or even distant places, God has a purpose for you. Matthew 28:19-20 *"Go and make disciples of all nations, baptizing them in the name of the Father and of the Son and of the Holy Spirit, and teaching them to obey everything I have commanded you."* Even if your mission field feels small, it matters to God. A kind word, a prayer, or sharing your testimony can change someone's life. Walking boldly in faith doesn't mean life will always be easy. The apostles faced persecution, imprisonment, and rejection. But they didn't give up because they trusted God. No matter what challenges you face—whether it's fear, doubt, or difficulties—God has already given you victory. You are not alone in your battles.

How The Holy Spirit Supercharges Believers To Live Boldly For God

The Holy Spirit is the third person of the Trinity—God the Father, God the Son (Jesus), and God the Holy Spirit. He is not just a force or a feeling but a person who lives in every believer. When we accept Jesus as our personal Lord and Savior, the Holy Spirit comes to live inside us to help us grow in faith and fulfill God's purpose for our lives. John 14:16-17, *"And I will ask the Father, and he will give you another advocate to help you and be with you forever—the Spirit of truth."* The Holy Spirit is our helper, teacher, and guide. Living boldly for God means standing firm in your faith, sharing the gospel without fear, and living in a way that reflects God's love and truth. It means stepping out of your comfort zone to follow God's will, even when it's challenging or unpopular. Boldness isn't about being loud or pushy—it's about having the courage to live according to God's Word and trusting Him fully, no matter what. Before Jesus went back to heaven, He told His disciples to wait for the Holy Spirit. He promised that the Spirit would give them the power they needed to spread the good news about Him. The same power that was given to the disciples is available to us today. The Holy Spirit gives us strength to face challenges, courage to speak about our faith, and the ability to live a godly life. Many people feel scared or unsure about sharing their faith. But the Holy Spirit gives us the words to say when we need them. Luke 12:12, *"For the Holy Spirit will teach you at that time what you should say."* Whether you're talking to a friend, a family member, or even a stranger, the Holy Spirit can guide your words and give you confidence.

Living for God isn't always easy. There will be times when we face challenges, opposition, or discouragement. The Holy Spirit is our source of strength during these times. The Holy Spirit doesn't just give us power; He also shows us the right path to take. He helps us make decisions that honor God and fulfill His purpose for our lives. John 16:13, *"But when he, the Spirit of truth, comes,*

he will guide you into all the truth." By spending time in prayer and reading God's Word, we can hear the Holy Spirit's voice and follow His direction. Prayer is a powerful way to connect with God, and the Holy Spirit helps us pray with boldness and faith. He also helps us when we don't know what to pray for. Romans 8:26 *"In the same way, the Spirit helps us in our weakness. We do not know what we ought to pray for, but the Spirit himself intercedes for us through wordless groans."* The Holy Spirit works in us to pray according to God's will, even when we don't have the right words. Fear is one of the biggest obstacles to living boldly for God. We might be afraid of what others will think or worried about failing. But the Holy Spirit replaces fear with courage and confidence. 2 Timothy 1:7 *"For the Spirit God gave us does not make us timid, but gives us power, love, and self-discipline."* With the Holy Spirit's help, we can overcome fear and step out in faith. The Holy Spirit works in us to make us more like Jesus. He helps us grow in love, joy, peace, patience, kindness, goodness, faithfulness, gentleness, and self-control—qualities known as the fruit of the Spirit. To live boldly for God, we need to be filled with the Holy Spirit. This means inviting Him to work in every part of our lives—our thoughts, actions, decisions, and relationships. When we live by the Holy Spirit, we can face each day with confidence, courage, and purpose. The Holy Spirit gives us the power to stand firm in our faith, share God's love with others, and live a life that honors Him.
With the Holy Spirit, we can live beyond our limits and do amazing things for God's glory.

Walking In Divine Authority To Impact Your World

When we talk about *divine authority*, we're talking about the power and permission God gives His children to act on His behalf. This authority doesn't come from our own strength or position —it comes from God through Jesus Christ. As believers, we are called not only to live in this authority but also to use it to make a difference in the world. Divine authority is the ability God gives to His people to carry out His will. It's not about control or domination; it's about being empowered by God to bring His love, truth, and power into the world. When Jesus rose from the dead, He declared in Matthew 28:18, *"All authority in heaven and on earth has been given to me."* Then He gave His followers this authority to continue His work on earth. Our authority comes from Jesus Christ. When we believe in Him, we are united with Him, and His power works through us. This means we don't need to be afraid of challenges, temptations, or spiritual battles because Jesus has given us the power to overcome.

This authority isn't something we earn—it's a gift from God. It's rooted in His Word, strengthened by His Spirit, and fueled by our faith. Walking in divine authority means living with confidence in God's promises. It means knowing who you are in Christ and standing firm in that identity. You can't walk in authority if you're disconnected from the One who gives it. Regular prayer, reading the Bible, and worshiping God keep you aligned with His will and empower you to act with His strength. The Bible is filled with promises and declarations of God's power. When you speak His Word over your life and situations, you are releasing His authority. Satan tries to deceive and discourage us, but we have authority to resist him. When you stand firm in God's truth, the enemy cannot overpower you.

Divine authority is not just for your personal benefit—it's meant to impact the world around you. God has placed you where you are to bring His Kingdom to earth. When you pray, remember that you are talking to the Creator of the universe. Your prayers have power. Pray boldly for your family, community, and the nations, asking God to bring healing, peace, and transformation. Your words have power. Use them to encourage, uplift, and share the truth of God's love. Whether you're speaking to a friend, a stranger, or a crowd, let your words reflect God's authority and compassion. God's authority is not just about speaking—it's about doing. Look for ways to serve others, whether it's helping someone in need, showing kindness to a neighbor, or volunteering in your community. Jesus used His authority to serve, and He calls us to do the same. One of the greatest ways to impact the world is by sharing the good news of Jesus. Walking in divine authority doesn't mean life will always be easy. You will face obstacles, but you don't have to face them alone. God has given you His Spirit to guide and strengthen you. When challenges come: Remind yourself of His Word, like Isaiah 54:17, *"No weapon formed against you shall prosper."* Trust that God is with you, even in the toughest times. Don't let fear or doubt stop you. With God's authority, you can overcome any obstacle. When you walk in God's authority, you become a light in the darkness. People will notice your peace, confidence, and love, and they will be drawn to God through you. Your actions and words can bring hope to the hopeless, healing to the hurting, and salvation to the lost. This power is not just for you—it's for the world. You don't have to wait for the perfect moment to start walking in divine authority. God has already given it to you through Jesus. Start today by trusting Him, speaking His Word, and stepping out in faith. Whether it's in your family, workplace, or community, God will use you to make an impact.

CHAPTER 14

BECOMING AN UNSTOPPABLE FORCE FOR GOD'S GLORY

God created you for more than just an ordinary life. You are not meant to simply go through the motions, staying comfortable or blending in. God has given you a purpose, a mission, and the power to live a life that glorifies Him and impacts the world. To live beyond the status quo means stepping into the extraordinary life God has planned for you. It means becoming an unstoppable force for His glory. The status quo means the way things are right now—living in a routine that feels comfortable, predictable, and safe. It often involves settling for what's easy or what is expected, without trying to do more or grow. Many people live this way, doing just enough to get by, staying within their comfort zones, and avoiding risks.

But God calls us to rise above the status quo. He created us for something greater than just an ordinary life. John 10:10 *"I have come that they may have life, and have it to the full."* This *full life* isn't about material wealth or personal achievements; it's about living with purpose, joy, and power as we serve God and fulfill His plans for us. It's about stepping into the extraordinary life He has designed, using His strength to rise above the ordinary. God doesn't want us to be stuck or limited—He wants us to grow, thrive, and make an impact for His kingdom. Living beyond the status quo starts with a shift in focus: making God's glory the ultimate goal of your life. To live for God's glory means that everything you do—your work, relationships, decisions, and even challenges—points back to how great and loving God is. It's about letting your life reflect His goodness so others are drawn to Him. When we live for God's glory, we shine like a light in a dark world. People can see God's love and power through our actions, words, and attitudes. But this requires surrender. You have to let go of your own plans and trust God to lead you. It means asking daily, "How can I honor God with my life today?" When you live for God's glory, you become unstoppable because God's power is working through you. The things that seemed impossible before now become possible, not because of your strength, but because of God's strength in you.

Fear and doubt are some of the biggest barriers to living beyond the status quo. Fear makes you worry about failing, being rejected, or facing the unknown.Doubt makes you question whether you're good enough, smart enough, or capable enough to follow God's plans.
Both fear and doubt can paralyze you, keeping you from stepping into the amazing life God has for you. But here's the truth: God hasn't given you a spirit of fear. He has equipped you with everything you need to overcome these challenges. Fear and doubt do not come from God. Instead, He gives you: Power to face challenges. Love to trust Him and care for others. Self-discipline to stay focused on His plans. When fear or doubt creeps in, remind yourself of God's promises. Declare that you are not alone, and God is with you every step of the way. To move beyond the status quo, you must have faith. Faith is trusting God, even when you don't see the full picture. It's believing that His plan is good and stepping out in obedience, even when it feels scary or uncertain. Hebrews 11:6, *"And without faith it is impossible to please God, because anyone who comes to him must believe that he exists and that he rewards those who earnestly seek him."* Faith isn't about waiting

until you have all the answers or feel ready. It's about taking the first step and trusting that God will guide the rest of the journey. Think about Peter walking on water in Matthew 14:29-31. He stepped out of the boat in faith, trusting Jesus to keep him afloat. Even though he became afraid, Jesus reached out and saved him. When you step out in faith, you: Open the door for God to work miracles in your life. Grow spiritually as you learn to depend on Him. Inspire others to trust God by your example. Faith takes you from an ordinary life to an extraordinary one, where you see God's power in action.

You cannot break free from the status quo and live for God's glory by your own strength. You need the power of the Holy Spirit. Courage to overcome fear. Wisdom to make godly decisions. Strength to face challenges and persevere. The Holy Spirit isn't just for big, extraordinary moments. He is with you every day, helping you in small ways and big ways to live boldly for God. When you rely on the Holy Spirit, you're no longer limited by your own abilities. God's unlimited power works through you, enabling you to: Share the Gospel with others. Overcome struggles and challenges. Make an impact in your family, community, and beyond. Living beyond the status quo means choosing to trust God for more—more purpose, more growth, and more impact. It means refusing to settle for what's easy and comfortable and instead stepping out in faith to fulfill God's plans. Recognize where you've been settling for less than God's best. Live in a way that honors Him and points others to His greatness. Trust God's promises and reject the lies that hold you back. Take action, even when you don't have all the answers. Let God's power work through you to accomplish things you could never do on your own. When you embrace this way of living, you experience the *full life* Jesus promised in John 10:10—a life filled with purpose, joy, and the satisfaction of knowing you are making an eternal difference. Trust God, step out, and watch Him transform your life and the lives of those around you.

Obstacles are a part of life. Everyone faces challenges, big or small. These obstacles can make us feel like giving up, but they are not meant to defeat us. In fact, with God by our side, we can overcome anything. Lean on God for strength. Don't try to handle everything by yourself. Trust that God is working behind the scenes, even when you don't see the solution yet. Keep going. Don't let setbacks stop you. With God, you can overcome anything. Remember, no matter how big the obstacle, God's power is bigger. He will help you overcome! Living for God's glory doesn't just affect you; it impacts those around you. Your life is a witness of His love and truth. Through your actions, words, and prayers, you have the ability to influence others for good. This command to share the Gospel and make disciples is not just for pastors or missionaries—it's for all believers. Each of us is called to share the love of Jesus in our own way, whether it's by encouraging a friend, serving in your community, or sharing the good news with someone who doesn't know Christ.
Impacting the world for God starts with. Being an example of His love. Show kindness, compassion, and forgiveness. Sharing your testimony. Let others know how God has changed your life. Actively serving others. Your service can be a powerful testimony of God's love. Remember, your life is a light to the world. Let it shine for God's glory.

To live beyond the status quo, you must be bold. Boldness doesn't mean being loud or aggressive; it means being courageous to do what's right, even when it's difficult. It means standing firm in your faith and not being afraid to share it with others, even when it's not popular. The Bible says in Proverbs 28:1: *"The righteous are as bold as a lion."* When you trust in God, He gives you the courage to face any situation with confidence. Boldness comes from knowing that you are not alone—God is with you. To live boldly: Speak up for what's right, even when it's hard. Stand firm in your beliefs, no matter what others say. Share your faith confidently, knowing that God is with you every step of the way. When you live for God's glory and walk in His purpose, nothing can stop you. You are empowered by the Holy Spirit, and God's strength is with you. Challenges may come, but with God, you are unstoppable. Romans 8:31, *"If God is for us, who can be against us?"* This is a powerful reminder that when God is on your side, no one or nothing can stand in your way. Your life, lived for God's purpose, will make an eternal impact. To become unstoppable: Keep walking in faith, trusting that God is with you. Stay committed to His purpose for your life, even when things get tough. Let the Holy Spirit guide you and empower you to do the impossible. Remember, when God is for you, there is no limit to what you can do. You are unstoppable in Him.

Developing The Mindset And Discipline To Be A World-Changer

Becoming a world-changer starts with your mindset and discipline. A world-changer is someone who makes a positive impact on others, influencing the world around them for good. As Christians, we are called to be world-changers for God's kingdom. But how do we develop the mindset and discipline to fulfill this calling? Let's break it down step by step. Before you can change the world, you need to know who you are in Christ. You are not just an ordinary person; you are a child of God, chosen and empowered by Him to make a difference. This understanding shapes your mindset. 1 Peter 2:9 *"But you are a chosen people, a royal priesthood, a holy nation, God's special possession, that you may declare the praises of him who called you out of darkness into his wonderful light."* When you know that God has called and chosen you, it gives you confidence to step out and make a difference. A world-changer doesn't settle for staying the same. You must have a growth mindset—a belief that you can learn, improve, and grow with God's help. Challenges and failures are not roadblocks; they are opportunities to grow stronger. Your mindset is shaped by what you focus on. To think like a world-changer, you need to fill your mind with God's truth and let it guide your thoughts and actions. This requires renewing your mind daily through prayer, reading the Bible, and meditating on God's promises. Big changes often start with small, consistent steps. Discipline is about doing the right thing even when it's hard or inconvenient. To be a world-changer, you need to be disciplined in your habits, like spending time with God, serving others, and pursuing excellence in what you do. 1 Corinthians 9:25, *"Everyone who competes in the games goes into strict training. They do it to get a crown that will not last, but we do it to get a crown that will last forever."* Just like an athlete trains for a race, you need to train yourself to stay focused and disciplined.

A world-changer has a clear vision of how they want to impact the world. Ask yourself, *"What has God called me to do? How can I make a difference?"* Your vision doesn't have to be huge at first. It could be making a difference in your family, church, or community. As you stay faithful, God will expand your influence. Habakkuk 2:2 *"Write down the revelation and make it plain on tablets so that a herald may run with it."* Having a clear vision helps you stay focused and motivated to keep moving forward. World-changers don't just focus on themselves—they focus on helping others. Jesus showed us this through His life. He served others with love and compassion, and He calls us to do the same. Mark 10:45, *"For even the Son of Man did not come to be served, but to serve, and to give his life as a ransom for many."* When you serve others, you reflect God's love and inspire change in the world. Making a difference often requires courage. You may face challenges, opposition, or fear, but God has not given you a spirit of fear. He has given you boldness to step out in faith. Trust that God is with you as you take bold steps to fulfill your calling.

Changing the world isn't easy. You may face setbacks, but don't give up. Perseverance is key to making a lasting impact. Trust that God will strengthen you to keep going. Galatians 6:9 *"Let us not become weary in doing good, for at the proper time we will reap a harvest if we do not give up."* Keep pressing on, knowing that your work for God is never in vain. To be a world-changer, you need God's power working in you. Stay connected to Him through prayer, worship, and reading His Word. He will guide you, strengthen you, and give you wisdom to make the right decisions. In John 15:5, *"I am the vine; you are the branches. If you remain in me and I in you, you will bear much fruit; apart from me you can do nothing."* When you rely on God, you will see His power at work in your life. A true world-changer doesn't work alone. Inspire others by living a life that reflects God's love, faith, and hope. Encourage people around you to join in making a positive impact. Together, we can accomplish more for God's kingdom. When others see your example, they will be encouraged to follow and make a difference too.

The Importance Of Staying Connected To God's Presence And Power

As Christians, one of the most important things in our lives is staying connected to God's presence and power. Just like a plant needs water and sunlight to grow, we need God's presence to thrive spiritually. When we stay close to God, we experience His love, peace, and strength. But when we distance ourselves from Him, we can feel lost, weak, and disconnected. One of the most powerful things about being close to God is the peace He gives. Life can be stressful and difficult, but God's presence brings calm to our hearts. When we stay close to Him, we can trust that He will help us through every situation. In His presence, we find comfort and assurance. When we pray and stay connected to God, His peace guards our hearts and minds, no matter what we are facing. God's power is always available to us, but we need to stay connected to Him to experience it. In times of weakness or struggle, God's power helps us to stand strong. His power gives us the strength to face challenges and to keep going when things seem tough. We can't do it on our own, but when we are connected to God, we can do anything with His help. Isaiah 40:29 *"He gives strength to the weary and increases the power of the weak."* When we feel tired or weak, God gives us His strength. We need to stay connected to Him so we can receive His power to keep moving forward. Staying close to God means we can hear His voice guiding us. Every day, we face decisions, big and small, and God wants to help us make the right choices. When we are connected to His presence, He can lead us through His Word, His Spirit, and through prayer. We are never alone when we stay connected to God—He is always there to guide us. When we trust God and stay connected to Him, He will lead us in the right direction.

Just like a tree needs water to grow, we need God's presence to grow spiritually. The more we stay connected to God, the more we become like Him. He helps us grow in love, patience, kindness, and every other good quality that reflects His nature. Staying close to God is how we grow stronger in our faith. John 15:5, *"I am the vine; you are the branches. If you remain in me and I in you, you will bear much fruit; apart from me you can do nothing."* When we stay connected to Jesus, we can grow and bear fruit, meaning our lives show God's goodness to others. Being close to God protects us from harm. In life, we face dangers, temptations, and difficult situations, but when we stay connected to God, He shields us with His protection. He watches over us and keeps us safe from things that could harm us, physically and spiritually. Psalm 91:1-2 *"Whoever dwells in the shelter of the Most High will rest in the shadow of the Almighty. I will say of the Lord, 'He is my refuge and my fortress, my God, in whom I trust.'"* When we stay in God's presence, we are safe in His care. He is our refuge and protector. When we are close to God, we experience His joy. This joy is not based on our circumstances, but on our relationship with Him. Even when things aren't perfect, we can still have joy because we know God is with us. His joy fills our hearts and gives us strength. Psalm 16:11 *"You make known to me the path of life; you will fill me with joy in your presence, with eternal pleasures at your right hand."* God's presence brings joy, and when we stay close to Him, He fills us with that joy. To stay connected to God, we need to make it a daily habit. Just like any relationship, it takes time and effort. We can stay connected to God through prayer, reading His Word, and spending time in worship. When we make time for God each day, we strengthen our relationship with Him, and we remain in His presence and power. James 4:8 *"Come near to God and he will come near to you."* This is a promise. When we take the step to draw near to God, He will draw near to us. It's a two-way relationship—God is always ready to be with us, but we need to choose to stay close to Him. When we stay connected to God, His presence changes us. The more time we spend with Him, the more we become like Him. He removes things in our lives that aren't good and replaces them with His peace, love, and grace. This transformation happens slowly but surely as we stay close to Him. 2 Corinthians 3:18 *"And we all, who with unveiled faces contemplate the Lord's glory, are being transformed into his image with ever-increasing glory, which comes from the Lord, who is the Spirit."* As we spend time in God's presence, we are transformed to be more like Jesus.

CONCLUSION

The Flight Of Faith

Faith is like the wings of an eagle, helping you soar higher in life. When you embrace the fullness of God's power, you can rise above challenges, doubts, and fears. Just like an eagle spreads its wings and takes flight, your faith can lift you above life's difficulties, guiding you to places you never imagined. The flight of faith is about trusting in God and allowing Him to carry you to new heights. It's not just about believing in God's existence—it's about having complete trust in His power, promises, and His plan for your life. This kind of faith gives you the strength to keep going, even when things are hard, and the courage to dream big.

In the Bible, **Isaiah 40:31** says, "But those who hope in the Lord will renew their strength. They will soar on wings like eagles; they will run and not grow weary, they will walk and not be faint." When we place our hope in God, He gives us the strength to soar —just like an eagle rising high in the sky. This is the kind of faith that helps us keep going, even when life gets tough. To soar higher in faith, you need to embrace the fullness of God's power. This means understanding that God is with you every step of the way, giving you the strength to face any challenge. When you truly believe in God's power, you are no longer held back by fear, doubt, or your own limitations. You can rise above them because you know that God is bigger than any problem you may face. With God's help, there are no limits to what we can achieve. His strength enables us to move beyond our own abilities and achieve great things for His glory. So, to soar higher in faith, start by relying on God's power, not just your own strength.

Faith is not just about believing in something; it's about acting on what you believe. If you truly have faith, you will take steps to follow God's plan for your life. Just like an eagle doesn't just sit in its nest but spreads its wings and flies, you must take action to move forward in your faith. One of the biggest obstacles to soaring in faith is fear and doubt. It's easy to be afraid of what might happen or to wonder if you are strong enough to face challenges. But remember, faith is the key that overcomes fear. 2 Timothy 1:7, "For God gave us a spirit not of fear but of power and love and self-control." When fear tries to hold you back, remember that God has given you power through His Holy Spirit. You can rise above fear and move forward in faith. Soaring in faith also means trusting God's timing. Sometimes we want things to happen quickly, but God's plans are often slower, but always perfect. The eagle waits for the right moment to spread its wings and take flight. Similarly, we must trust that God knows the best time to move us forward in our journey. Ecclesiastes 3:1, "There is a time for everything, and a season for every activity under the heavens." Trust that God will lift you at the right moment, and that He is preparing you for something great. The flight of faith calls you to rise above just going through the motions of everyday life. It invites you to live with purpose, to trust that God has more for you, and to take bold steps toward His plans. Soaring in faith means you don't settle for what's comfortable or familiar. You trust God to take you higher, into new possibilities and experiences. Ephesians 3:20, "Now to him who is able to do immeasurably more than all we ask or imagine, according to his power that is at work within us." This verse that God is able to do far more than we could ever dream or imagine. When you have faith, you open yourself up to receive all that God has for you—things that you may never have thought possible. As you embrace the fullness of God's power, you will experience joy in your journey. Soaring in faith brings peace, confidence, and fulfillment. It's a journey that may have challenges, but it's also filled with the excitement of discovering new things about God and His plan for your life. Each time you rise above a difficulty, your faith grows stronger, and you become more confident in God's ability to carry you through.

The eagle, when It soars high In the sky, Is free from the ground below. Similarly, when you soar in faith, you experience the freedom that comes with trusting God fully. This freedom isn't just in physical situations—it's a peace that fills your heart, knowing that God is in control.

When you decide to follow Jesus and live for Him, your life becomes a new journey filled with purpose, power, and passion. As a believer, you are not just living a normal life. You are called to make a difference in the world, to impact nations, and to bring God's kingdom to earth. This journey might seem big, but remember, it's a journey that God has already prepared for you, and He equips you every step of the way. A "supercharged" believer is someone who has received the power and strength of the Holy Spirit. This power comes from God, not from our own strength, and it helps us do things we could never do on our own. The moment you accepted Jesus into your life, the Holy Spirit began working in you, making you stronger and more capable of doing God's work on earth. In Acts 1:8, Jesus promised, "But you will receive power when the Holy Spirit comes on you; and you will be my witnesses in Jerusalem, and in all Judea and Samaria, and to the ends of the earth." This power is not just for your own benefit—it's for spreading God's message, helping others, and bringing His love and truth to everyone you meet. As a supercharged believer, you are empowered to live boldly, to overcome challenges, and to step out in faith, knowing that God is with you. You carry His presence, and that presence is powerful.

God has called you to more than just living a quiet, everyday life.

He has called you to impact nations. This might sound like a big task, but God works through people just like you to change the world. In Matthew 28:19, Jesus gave a command to His followers: "Go and make disciples of all nations." This means that no matter where you are—whether in your home, your workplace, your school, or traveling abroad—you are called to share God's love and His message of salvation. You might be thinking, "I am just one person. How can I make a difference in the whole world?" The truth is, you don't have to do it all by yourself. God has a plan for you, and He will guide your steps. You may not travel to every nation, but through your prayers, actions, and influence, you can reach people far beyond where you live. The impact you have can be through small acts of kindness, sharing your testimony, serving others, or even using your skills and talents to help bring God's kingdom to earth. 2 Corinthians 5:20, "We are therefore Christ's ambassadors, as though God were making his appeal through us." You ar" an ambassador for Christ, representing His kingdom and His love wherever you go. What does it mean to bring God's kingdom to earth? The kingdom of God is where God's will is done—where His love, peace, justice, and righteousness rule. When you bring God's kingdom to earth, you are allowing God's power to be shown in your life and in the world around you. In Matthew 6:10, when Jesus taught His disciples how to pray, He said, "Your kingdom come, your will be done, on earth as it is in heaven." This is a prayer for God's kingdom to be visible in the world. As believers, we are called to make this prayer a reality by living out God's values in everything we do. This means living with love, kindness, integrity, and truth in your everyday life.

As you live out God's love and purpose, you will see His kingdom grow through you. Telling others about Jesus and His love is one of the most powerful ways to bring God's kingdom to earth. When people accept Jesus into their hearts, they become part of God's kingdom. The kingdom of God is a kingdom of love. By showing love to others, especially those who are hurting or in need, you reflect God's heart. Jesus said in John 13:34, "A new command I give you: Love one another. As I have loved you, so you must love one another."

In a world that can sometimes be full of dishonesty, living a life of truth and integrity is a way to reflect God's kingdom. In Matthew 5:14, Jesus said, "You are the light of the world. A town built on a hill cannot be hidden." Your honesty and goodness can be a light in the darkness. When you help the poor, the sick, and the oppressed, you bring God's kingdom to earth. In Matthew 25:40, Jesus said, "Truly I tell you, whatever you did for one of the least of these brothers and sisters of mine, you did for me." Serving others is one of the ways to show God's love and care for the world.

As a supercharged believer, your journey is also powered by prayer and faith. Prayer connects you to God, and it's through prayer that you receive direction, strength, and peace. Faith is what keeps you going, even when things are tough. It is faith in God's promises and His plan for your life. You trust that He is working all things for your good, and that He will empower you to do the work He has called you to do. One of the keys to impacting nations and bringing God's kingdom to earth is boldness. As a supercharged believer, you have been given the courage and confidence to step out and do what God calls you to do. In Acts 4:29, the early believers prayed, "Now, Lord, consider their threats and enable your servants to speak your word with great boldness." Don't be afraid to speak up for Jesus. Don't be afraid to make a difference in your community. The Holy Spirit inside of you is your source of boldness, and He will guide you in every step. On this journey of impacting nations and bringing God's kingdom to earth, remember that you are not alone. God is with you, and He has given you the Holy Spirit to guide and empower you. You are part of a larger family of believers around the world, all working together to fulfill God's mission. Matthew 28:20 promises, "And surely I am with you always, to the very end of the age." Your new journey as a supercharged believer is about embracing your role in God's big plan. You are called to be a light in the world, to impact the nations, and to bring God's kingdom to earth. Through the power of the Holy Spirit, your actions, words, and prayers can make a lasting difference. Step out in boldness, live out your faith, and trust that God will use you to change the world. Your journey is just beginning, and as you follow God's lead, you will see His kingdom grow and His will done on earth as it is in heaven. This is about rising above the status quo, stepping out in trust, and embracing the fullness of God's power. It's about allowing God to carry you to new heights and experiences as you live out His purpose for your life. So, spread your wings of faith, trust in God's power, and watch as He helps you soar higher than you ever thought possible. Remember, with God, all things are possible, and as you continue to trust in Him, you'll rise above any challenges and experience the freedom of living out His plans for you.

A SPECIAL CALL TO SALVATION & NEW BEGINNINGS FROM APOSTLE DR. DAVID PHILEMON

Dear Beloved,

God loves you deeply and has brought you to this moment for a reason. No matter your past, His love and forgiveness are available to you.

The Bible says in John 3:16, "For God so loved the world that He gave His one and only Son, that whoever believes in Him shall not perish but have eternal life." Jesus Christ came to save you, offering you a new life of purpose and peace.

If you're ready to accept Jesus as your Lord and Savior, pray this simple prayer:

The Salvation Prayer

"Heavenly Father, I come to You in the Name of Jesus. I acknowledge that I am a sinner in need of a Savior. I believe that

Jesus Christ is Your Son, that He died for my sins, and that You raised Him from the dead. I repent of my sins and turn to You with my

Whole heart. Jesus, I ask You to come into my life. Be my Lord and my Savior. I surrender my life to You. Fill me with Your Holy Spirit, guide me on the path of righteousness, and help me to follow Your script for my life. Thank you, Father, for saving me. In the name of Jesus. Amen."

Welcome to the Family of God!

If you have just prayed this prayer, Congratulations! You are now a child of God, and heaven is rejoicing. Your journey has begun, and we're here to support you as you grow in faith and discover God's unique plans for you.

Next Steps:

- Connect with a Bible-believing church.

- Read the Bible Daily: God's Word is your guide.

- Pray Regularly: Prayer is your lifeline to God.

- Share Your Faith: Don't keep the good news to yourself.

APPENDIX

1. Prayer For Deliverance From Strongholds

Scripture: *2 Corinthians 10:4-5* "For the weapons of our warfare are not carnal but mighty in God for pulling down strongholds, casting down arguments and every high thing that exalts itself against the knowledge of God."

Prayer: Heavenly Father, I come before You in the name of Jesus, asking You to break every stronghold that has been established in my life. I pull down every argument, every lie, and every high thing that tries to exalt itself against Your knowledge. I claim victory in every area where I have been bound by the enemy's plans. Lord, deliver me from all spiritual bondage, and let Your power manifest in my life to bring freedom and breakthrough. I stand on Your Word, knowing that the weapons You have given me are mighty for pulling down strongholds. In Jesus' name, Amen.

2. Prayer For Overcoming Obstacles And Breaking Barriers

Scripture: *Matthew 17:20* "If you have faith as small as a mustard seed, you can say to this mountain, 'Move from here to there,' and it will move. Nothing will be impossible for you."

Prayer: Father God, I thank You for the gift of faith, even if it is as small as a mustard seed. I speak to every mountain of difficulty, every obstacle, and every barrier in my life, and I command them to move in the name of Jesus. Nothing is impossible for You, and I trust that You are making a way where there seems to be no way. I stand in faith, knowing that You are my deliverer and that through Your power, I will overcome. In Jesus' name, Amen.

3. Prayer For Restoration And Family Deliverance

Scripture: *Joel 2:25* "I will repay you for the years the locusts have eaten—the great locust and the young locust, the other locusts and the locust swarm—my great army that I sent among you."

Prayer: Lord, I thank You for the promise of restoration in my life. I bring before You every area of my family that has been affected by the enemy's attacks. I ask You to restore what has been lost, heal broken relationships, and deliver my loved ones from every stronghold. I claim the promise that You will repay us for the years the locusts have eaten, and I trust that You will restore our family to the place of abundance and peace. In Jesus' name, Amen.

4. Prayer For Spiritual Empowerment And Boldness

Scripture: *Acts 1:8* "But you will receive power when the Holy Spirit comes on you; and you will be my witnesses in Jerusalem, and in all Judea and Samaria, and to the ends of the earth."

Prayer: Holy Spirit, I invite You into my life today. Empower me with Your power to be a bold witness for Christ in every area of my life. Fill me with courage to speak the truth, to walk in faith, and to do the works You have called me to do. I claim the promise of Acts 1:8, that Your power will come upon me and transform me into an unstoppable force for Your kingdom. Use me, Lord, to impact my community and the world for Your glory. In Jesus' name, Amen.

5. Prayer For Victory Over Spiritual Battles

Scripture: *Ephesians 6:10-12* "Finally, be strong in the Lord and in His mighty power. Put on the full armor of God, so that you can take your stand against the devil's schemes. For our struggle is not against flesh and blood, but against the rulers, against the authorities, against the powers of this dark world and against the spiritual forces of evil in the heavenly realms."

Prayer: Lord, I thank You for the strength and power You provide to overcome spiritual battles. I put on the full armor of God today, knowing that I am not fighting against flesh and blood, but against spiritual forces that seek to hinder my purpose. I stand firm in Your mighty power, and I declare that no weapon formed against me shall prosper. Protect my mind, heart, and spirit as I wage this battle, and give me the wisdom to recognize the enemy's schemes. I trust in Your victory and will walk in it today. In Jesus' name, Amen.

6. Prayer For The Restoration Of God's Voice In My Life

Scripture: *1 Samuel 3:10* "The Lord came and stood there, calling as at the other times, 'Samuel! Samuel!' Then Samuel said, 'Speak, for your servant is listening.'"

Prayer: Heavenly Father, I come before You, asking that You restore Your voice in my life. I want to hear You clearly, just as Samuel heard You in the quiet of the night. Speak to me, Lord, for Your servant is listening. Remove every distraction, every block that prevents me from hearing Your voice, and lead me with Your divine guidance. I surrender my heart and mind to You, trusting that You will speak to me and guide me on the path You have set before me. In Jesus' name, Amen.

7. Prayer For Breakthrough In Health And Healing

Scripture: *Isaiah 53:5* "But He was pierced for our transgressions, He was crushed for our iniquities; the punishment that brought us peace was on Him, and by His wounds we are healed."

Prayer: Lord, I thank You for the healing power that was made available to me through the sacrifice of Jesus Christ. I claim healing in my body, mind, and spirit today. By the wounds of Jesus, I am healed. I reject every sickness, pain, and affliction, and I receive Your healing and breakthrough in every area of my life. Let Your healing power flow through me, restoring me to full health and vitality. In Jesus' name, Amen.

8. Prayer For Supernatural Empowerment And Strength

Scripture: *Philippians 4:13* "I can do all things through Christ who strengthens me."

Prayer: Father, I thank You that You have given me the strength to overcome any challenge. I declare that through Christ, I can do all things. Empower me to rise above every obstacle, every trial, and every difficulty. Strengthen my faith, my mind, and my spirit so that I can live victoriously and fulfill Your purpose for my life. I trust that You will give me the strength to soar, knowing that I can do all things through You. In Jesus' name, Amen.

ABOUT THE BOOK

"Supercharged to Soar" is a powerful and inspiring guide designed to help you break free from limitations and walk in the fullness of your God-given potential. This book is a call to believers to rise above every challenge, obstacle, and setback, empowering them to step into their divine purpose and soar to new heights. Through biblical principles and practical applications, this book provides a roadmap for spiritual, emotional, and personal breakthrough. "Supercharged to Soar" offers clear, actionable steps for overcoming strongholds, breaking barriers, and experiencing the freedom and power available to every believer through Jesus Christ. This book explores the following key themes:

- Deliverance and Breakthrough
- Empowerment Through Faith
- Spiritual Victory
- Restoration and Healing
- Living with Purpose

"Supercharged to Soar" is for anyone who is tired of being stuck, feeling defeated, or not living up to their full potential. It's time to rise up, break free from every chain, and soar into the abundant life that God has promised. With God's help, your best days are ahead, and this book will equip you with the strength, wisdom, and faith to reach new heights in every area of your life.

www.ingramcontent.com/pod-product-compliance
Lightning Source LLC
Chambersburg PA
CBHW062111080426
42734CB00012B/2823